DEVELOPING
the LEADERS
AROUND YOU

DEVELOPING
the LEADERS
AROUND YOU

JOHN C. MAXWELL

THOMAS NELSON
Since 1798

NASHVILLE DALLAS MEXICO CITY RIO DE JANEIRO BEIJING

Published in Nashville, Tennessee, by Thomas Nelson. Thomas Nelson is a registered trademark of Thomas Nelson, Inc.

Thoma Nelson, Inc., titles may be purchased in bulk for educational, business, fund-raising, or sales promotional use. For information, please e-mail SpecialMarkets@ThomasNelson.com.

Library of Congress Cataloging-in-Publication Data

Maxwell, John C., 1947–
    Developing the leaders around you / John C. Maxwell
      p. cm.
    Includes bibliographical references.
    ISBN 0-7852-6198-2 (IE)
    ISBN 978-07852-6150-6 (HC)
    ISBN 978-0-7852-8111-5 (TP)
    1. Leadership. I. Title.
    HD57.7.M39423 1995
    658.4'092—dc20   94-42608
                                                    CIP

Printed in the United States of America

09 10 11 12   RRD   17 16

This book is dedicated to the men who have developed me:

To Larry Maxwell,
my brother, who encouraged in me the desire
to grow mentally;

To Glenn Leatherwood,
my junior high Sunday school teacher,
who inspired me to have a heart for God;

To my high school basketball coach,
Don Neff, who instilled in me the desire to win;

To Elmer Towns, pastor and friend,
who strengthened my desire to reach my potential;

And above all, to my father, Melvin Maxwell,
my lifelong mentor. I am a leader today because of the time
you spent developing me.

CONTENTS

CONTENTS

ONE

THE LEADER'S KEY QUESTION:
AM I RAISING UP POTENTIAL LEADERS?

One night, after working quite late, I grabbed a copy of *Sports Illustrated*, hoping its pages would lull me to sleep. It had the opposite effect. On the back cover was an advertisement that caught my eye and got my emotional juices flowing. It featured a picture of John Wooden, the coach who led the UCLA Bruins for many years. The caption beneath his picture read, "The guy who puts the ball through the hoop has ten hands."

John Wooden was a great basketball coach. Called "the Wizard of Westwood," he brought ten national basketball championships to UCLA in a span of twelve years. Two back-to-back championships are almost unheard of in the world of competitive sports, but he led the Bruins to *seven titles in a row*. It took a consistent level of superior play, good coaching, and hard practice. But the key to the Bruins's success was Coach Wooden's unyielding dedication to his concept of teamwork.

He knew that if you oversee people and you wish to develop leaders, you are responsible to: (1) appreciate them for who they are; (2) believe that they will do their very best; (3) praise their accomplishments; and (4) accept your personal responsibility to them as their leader.

Coach Bear Bryant expressed this same sentiment when he said:

> I'm just a plowhand from Arkansas, but I have learned how to hold a team together—how to lift some men up, how to calm others down, until finally they've got one heartbeat together as a team. There's always just three things I say: "If anything goes bad, I did it. If anything goes semi-good, then we did it. If anything goes real good, they did it." That's all it takes to get people to win.

Bear Bryant won people and games. Until a few years ago, he held the title of the winningest coach in the history of college football with 323 victories.

Great leaders—the truly successful ones who are in the top 1 percent—all have one thing in common. They know that acquiring and keeping good people is a leader's most important task. An organization cannot increase its productivity—but people can! The asset that truly appreciates within any organization is people. Systems become dated. Buildings deteriorate. Machinery wears. But people can grow, develop, and become more effective if they have a leader who understands their potential value.

> **Acquiring and keeping good people is a leader's most important task.**

The bottom line—and the essential message of this book—is that you can't do it alone. If you really want to be a successful leader, you must develop other leaders around you. You must establish a team. You must find a way to get your vision seen, implemented, and contributed to by others. The leader sees the big picture, but he needs other leaders to help make his mental picture a reality.

Jesus

Most leaders have followers around them. They believe the key to leadership is gaining more followers. Few leaders surround themselves with other leaders, but the ones who do bring great value to their organizations. And not only is their burden lightened, but their vision is also carried on and enlarged.

WHY LEADERS NEED TO REPRODUCE LEADERS

The key to surrounding yourself with other leaders is to find the best people you can, then develop them into the best leaders they can be. Great leaders produce other leaders. Let me tell you why:

THOSE CLOSEST TO THE LEADER WILL DETERMINE THE SUCCESS LEVEL OF THAT LEADER

The greatest leadership principle that I have learned in more than thirty years of leadership is that those closest to the leader will determine the success level of that leader. A negative reading of this statement is also true: Those closest to the leader will determine the level of failure for that leader. In other words, the people close to me "make me or break me." The determination of a positive or negative outcome in my leadership depends upon my ability as a leader to develop those closest to me. It also depends upon my ability to recognize the value that others bring to my organization. My goal is not to draw a following that results in a crowd. My goal is to develop leaders who become a movement.

Stop for a moment and think of the five or six people closest to you in your organization. Are you developing them? Do you have a game plan for them? Are they growing? Have they been able to lift your load?

Within my organizations leadership development is continually emphasized. In their first training session, I give new leaders this principle: *As a potential leader you are either an asset or a liability to the organization.* I illustrate this truth by saying, "When there's a problem, a 'fire' in the organization, you as a leader are often the first to arrive at the scene. You have in your hands two buckets. One contains water and the other contains gasoline. The 'spark' before you will either become a greater problem because you pour the gasoline on it, or it will be extinguished because you use the bucket of water."

Every person within your organization also carries two buckets. The question a leader needs to ask is, "Am I training them to use the gasoline or the water?"

AN ORGANIZATION'S GROWTH POTENTIAL IS DIRECTLY RELATED TO ITS PERSONNEL POTENTIAL

When conducting leadership conferences, I often make the statement, "Grow a leader—grow the organization." A company cannot grow without until its leaders grow within.

> Grow a leader—grow the organization.

I am often amazed at the amount of money, energy, and marketing focus organizations spend on areas that will not produce growth. Why advertise that the customer is number one when the personnel have not been trained in customer service? When customers arrive, they will know the difference between an employee who has been trained to give service and one who hasn't. Slick brochures and catchy slogans will never overcome incompetent leadership.

In 1981 I became Senior Pastor of Skyline Wesleyan Church in San Diego, California. This congregation averaged 1,000 in attendance from 1969 to 1981, and it was on an obvious plateau. When I assumed leadership responsibilities, the first question I asked was, "Why has the growth stopped?" I needed to find an answer, so I called my first staff meeting and gave a lecture titled *The Leadership Line.* My thesis was, "Leaders determine the level of an organization." I drew a line across a marker board and wrote the number "1,000." I shared with the staff that for thirteen years the average attendance at Skyline was 1,000. I knew the staff could lead 1,000 people effectively. What I did not know was whether they could lead 2,000 people. So I drew a dotted line and wrote the number 2,000, and I placed a question mark between the two lines. I then drew an arrow from the bottom 1,000 to the top 2,000 line and wrote the word "change."

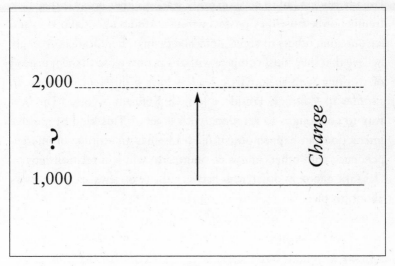

It would be my responsibility to train them and help them make the necessary changes to reach our new goal. When the leaders changed positively, I knew the growth would become automatic. Now, I had to help them change themselves, or I knew I would literally have to change them by hiring others to take their place.

From 1981 to 1995 I gave this lecture at Skyline on three occasions. The last time, the number 4,000 was placed on the top line. As I discovered, the numbers changed, but the lecture didn't. The

> **Everything rises and falls on leadership.**

strength of any organization is a direct result of the strength of its leaders. Weak leaders equal weak organizations. Strong leaders equal strong organizations. Everything rises and falls on leadership.

POTENTIAL LEADERS HELP CARRY THE LOAD

Businessman Rolland Young said, "I am a self-made man, but I think if I had it to do over again, I would call in someone else!" Usually leaders fail to develop other leaders either because they lack training or because they possess wrong attitudes about allowing and encouraging others to come alongside them. Often, leaders wrongly believe that they must compete with the people close to them instead of working with them. Great leaders have a different mind-set. In *Profiles in Courage*, President John F. Kennedy wrote, "The best way to go along is to get along with others." This kind of positive interaction can happen only if the leader has an attitude of interdependency with others and is committed to win-win relationships.

Take a look at differences between the two views leaders possess about people:

WINNING BY COMPETITIVENESS	WINNING BY COOPERATION
Look at others as enemies	Look at others as friends
Concentrate on yourself	Concentrate on others
Become suspicious of others	Become supportive of others
Win only if you are good	Win if you or others are good
Winning determined by your skills	Winning determined by the skills of many

Small victory	Large victory
Some joy	Much joy
There are winners and losers	There are only winners

Peter Drucker was correct when he said, "No executive has ever suffered because his people were strong and effective." The leaders around me lift my load in many ways. Here are two of the most important ones:

1. *They become a sounding board for me.* As a leader, I sometimes hear counsel that I don't want to hear but need to hear. That's the advantage of having leaders around you—having people who know how to make decisions. Followers tell you what you want to hear. Leaders tell you what you need to hear.

I have always encouraged those closest to me to give me advice on the front end. In other words, an opinion before a decision has potential value. An opinion after the decision has been made is worthless. Alex Agase, a college football coach, once said, "If you really want to give me advice, do it on Saturday afternoon between one and four o'clock, when you've got twenty-five seconds to do it, between plays. Don't give me advice on Monday. I know the right thing to do on Monday."

2. *They possess a leadership mind-set.* Fellow leaders do more than work with the leader, they think like the leader. It gives them the power to lighten the load. This becomes invaluable in areas such as decision making, brainstorming, and providing security and direction to others.

A majority of my time is spent away from the office speaking at conferences and events. Therefore, it is essential that I have leaders in my organizations who can carry on effectively while I am gone. And they do. It happens because I have spent my life finding and developing potential leaders. The results are very gratifying.

This leadership mind-set of sharing the load is wonderfully demonstrated by, of all things, geese, as illustrated by Tom Worsham:

When you see geese heading south for the winter flying along in a "V" formation, you might be interested in knowing that science has discovered why they fly that way. Research has revealed that as each bird flaps its wings, it creates an uplift for the bird immediately behind it. By flying in a "V" formation, the whole flock adds at least 71 percent greater flying range than if each bird flew on its own. (*People who share a common direction and sense of community get where they are going more quickly and easily because they are traveling on one another's thrust.*)

Whenever a goose falls out of formation, it suddenly feels the drag and resistance of trying to go it alone. It quickly gets back into formation to take advantage of the lifting power of the bird immediately in front. (*If we as people have as much sense as a goose, we will stay in formation and so will those who are headed the same way we are.*) When the lead goose gets tired, he rotates back in the "V" and another goose flies the point. (*It pays to take turns doing hard jobs.*)

The geese honk from behind to encourage those up front to keep up their speed. (*What do we say when we honk from behind?*)

And finally, when a goose gets sick, or is wounded by gunfire and falls out, two other geese fall out of formation and follow it down to help and protect it. They stay with the goose until it is either able to fly again or dead, and then they launch out on their own or with another formation to catch up with their group. (*If we have the sense of a goose, we will stand by each other like that.*)

Whoever was the first to call another person a "silly goose" didn't know enough about geese![1]

LEADERS ATTRACT POTENTIAL LEADERS

Birds of a feather really do flock together. I really believe that it takes a leader to know a leader, grow a leader, and show a leader. I have also found that it takes a leader to attract a leader.

Attraction is the obvious first step, yet I find many people in leadership positions who are unable to accomplish this task. True leaders are able to attract potential leaders because:

- Leaders think like them.

- Leaders express feelings that other leaders sense.

- Leaders create an environment that attracts potential leaders.

- Leaders are not threatened by people with great potential.

For example, a person in a leadership position who is a "5" on a scale of 1 to 10 will not attract a leader who is a "9." Why? Because leaders naturally size up any crowd and migrate to other leaders who are at the same or higher level.

Any leader who has only followers around him will be called upon to continually draw on his own resources to get things done. Without other leaders to carry the load, he will become fatigued and burnt out. Have you asked yourself lately, "Am I tired?" If the answer is yes, you may have a good reason for it, as this humorous story illustrates:

> It takes a leader to know a leader, grow a leader, and show a leader.

Somewhere in the world there is a country with a population of 220 million. Eighty-four million are over sixty years of age, which leaves 136 million to do the work. People under twenty years of age total 95 million, which leaves 41 million to do the work.

There are 22 million employed by the government, which leaves 19 million to do the work. Four million are in the Armed Forces, which leaves 15 million to do the work. Deduct 14,800,000, the number in state and city offices, and that leaves 200,000 to do the work. There are 188,000 in hospitals or insane asylums, so that leaves 12,000 to do the work.

It is of interest to note that in this country 11,998 people are in jail, so that leaves just two people to carry the load. That's you and me—and brother, I'm getting tired of doing everything myself!

Unless you want to carry the whole load yourself, you need to be developing leaders.

LEADERS WHO MENTOR POTENTIAL LEADERS MULTIPLY THEIR EFFECTIVENESS

Not long ago, at a conference where management expert Peter Drucker was speaking, thirty of my leaders and I were continually challenged to produce and mentor other leaders. Peter asked us, "Who will take your place?" He kept emphasizing, "There is no success without a successor."

I left that meeting with one resolve: *I was going to produce leaders who could produce other leaders.* No longer was it enough to grow by adding leaders. Now, my focus was upon *multiplying* those leaders. To accomplish this, I began to train my leaders to learn the fine art of setting parameters and priorities. I wanted them to gain a deep understand of our goals and then go out into our

organization and train others to someday re-
place them or help carry the load.

At that time, the board of my organization became my focus for developing leaders. In 1989 one-half of my board members

> **There is no success without a successor.**

were brand new, and the group faced major decisions on a $35 mil-
lion relocation project. I was concerned. Could decisions of such
magnitude be made by rookies? However, my fears subsided at the
next board retreat when I discovered that every new board member
had been mentored by former, experienced members. The old board
had heard me and implemented my teachings, and the new board
was now benefiting. The new members had come into their positions already running with the rest of us. It was then that I realized
an important lesson: *Leaders create and inspire new leaders by
instilling faith in their leadership abilities and helping them develop
and hone leadership skills they don't know they possess.*

My experience with the board shows what happens when people
work together—side by side. When people work for a common
cause, they no longer *add* to their growth potential. Their unity *multiplies* their strength. The following anecdote further illustrates my
point:

At a Midwestern fair, many spectators gathered for an old-
fashioned horse pull (an event where various weights are put on
a horse-drawn sled and pulled along the ground). The grand-
champion horse pulled a sled with 4,500 pounds on it. The runner-
up was close, with a 4,400-pound pull. Some of the men wondered
what the two horses could pull if hitched together. Separately they
totaled nearly 9,000 pounds, but when hitched and working
together as a team, they pulled over 12,000 pounds.

DEVELOPED LEADERS EXPAND AND ENHANCE THE FUTURE OF THE ORGANIZATION

I was once asked to speak at a conference on the subject, *How to Structure Your Organization for Growth*. I politely refused. I am convinced that structure can aid growth but not give it. Pollster George Barna said, "Great organizations may have great leaders and a poor structure, but I've never seen a great organization that had a great structure and a poor leader." Structure can mean the difference between a bad organization and a good one. But the difference between a good organization and a great one is leadership.

Henry Ford knew this. He said, "You can take my factories, burn up my buildings, but give me my people, and I'll bring my business right back again." What did Henry Ford know that so many other people in leadership positions don't know? He knew that buildings and bureaucracy are not essential to growth. A company must organize around what it is trying to accomplish, not around what is being done. I have seen people in an organization do things a particular way simply because the bureaucracy states it must be done that way, even when it hinders what the organization is trying to accomplish. Organize around tasks, not functions.

Too often we are like the community that built a new bridge:

The residents of a small town built a new bridge. Then they decided that, if they had a new bridge, they'd better hire a watchman to keep an eye on it. So they did. Someone noted that the watchman needed a salary, so they hired an accountant. He in turn pointed out the need for a treasurer. With a watchman, an accountant, and a treasurer, they had to have an administrator, so residents appointed one. Congress then voted a cut in funding, and personnel had to be cut back. So, they fired the watchman!

Don't let the machinations or trappings of your organization make you lose sight of what's to be accomplished.

One of the things my father taught me was the importance of people above all other elements in an organization. He was the president of a college for sixteen years. One day, as we sat on a campus bench, he explained that the most expensive workers on campus were not the highest paid. The most expensive ones were the people who were nonproductive. He explained that developing leaders took time and cost money. You usually had to pay leaders more. But such people were an invaluable asset. They attracted a higher quality of person; they were more productive; and they continued to add value to the organization. He closed the conversation by saying, "Most people produce only when they feel like it. Leaders produce even when they don't feel like it."

THE MORE PEOPLE YOU LEAD, THE MORE LEADERS YOU NEED

Moses was the greatest leader in the Old Testament. How would you like to relocate one-and-a-half million complaining people? It was hard . . . and tiring. And as his nation grew, Moses became more tired, and the people's needs went unmet.

The problem? Moses was trying to do it all himself. His *Disorganization Chart* looked like the diagram on page 14.

Jethro, the father-in-law of Moses, suggested that he find, recruit, and train other leaders to assist him in his leadership responsibilities. Moses followed that advice, and soon he had other leaders helping him carry the load. The result? This needed change gave added strength to Moses and enabled all the needs of the people to be met.

> A leader's success can be defined as the maximum utilization of the abilities of those under him.

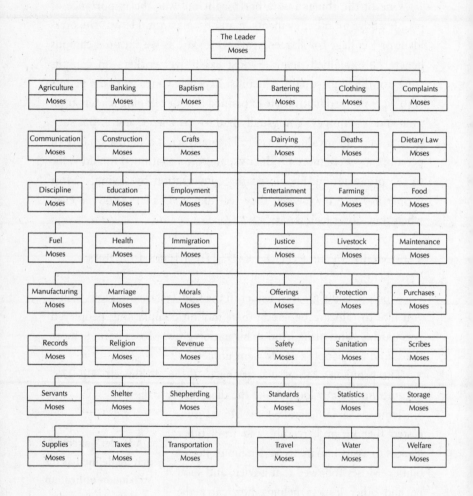

Zig Ziglar says, "Success is the maximum utilization of the ability that you have." I believe a leader's success can be defined as *the maximum utilization of the abilities of those under him.* Andrew Carnegie explained it like this: "I wish to have as my epitaph: 'Here lies a man who was wise enough to bring into his service men who knew more than he.'" It is my desire that the following pages help you do exactly that.

<hr>

TWO

THE LEADER'S TOUGHEST CHALLENGE:
CREATING A CLIMATE FOR POTENTIAL LEADERS

Those who believe in our abilities do more than stimulate us—they create an atmosphere in which it becomes easier for us to succeed. Creating an environment that will attract leaders is vital to any organization. Doing that is the job of leaders. They must be active; they must generate activity that is productive; and they must encourage, create, and command changes in the organization. They must create a climate in which potential leaders will thrive.

LEADERS MUST BE ENVIRONMENTAL CHANGE AGENTS

The leaders in any organization must be the environmental change agents. They must be more like thermostats than thermometers. At first glance, a person could confuse these instruments. Both are capable of measuring heat. However, they are really quite different. A thermometer is passive. It records the temperature of its environment but can do nothing to change that environment. A thermostat is an active instrument. It determines what the environment will be. It effects change in order to create a climate.

The attitude of the leader, coupled with a positive atmosphere in the organization, can encourage people to accomplish great things. And consistent accomplishment generates momentum. Many times momentum is the only difference between a winning, positive growth climate and a losing, negative growth climate.

Leaders cannot afford to overlook the importance of momentum:

With momentum,	Leaders look better than they actually are.
With momentum,	Followers increase their performance.
Without momentum,	Leaders look worse than they actually are.
Without momentum,	Followers decrease their performance.

Momentum is the greatest of all change agents. More than 90 percent of the successful changes we've instituted in our organization have been the result of creating momentum before asking people to change.

To maximize the *value* of momentum, leaders must: (1) develop an appreciation for it *early*; (2) know the key ingredients of it *immediately*; and (3) pour resources into it *always*.

The next time you find it difficult to adjust the environment in your company, keep in mind this simple fact from the laws of physics:

Indictor: What is our momentum?
- New + Spirit
- New leadership change
- goals

Water boils at 212 degrees, but at 211 degrees, it is still just hot water. One extra degree, an increase of less than one-half of one percent, can make the difference between a pot of languishing liquid and a bubbling caldron of power. One degree can create a full head of steam—enough power to move a train weighing tons. That one degree is usually momentum.

> **Momentum is the greatest of all change agents.**

Leaders in some organizations don't recognize the importance of creating a climate conducive to building potential leaders. They don't understand how it works. Advertising executive William Bernbach, who understands the difference it makes, once stated, "I'm always amused when other agencies try to hire my people away. They'd have to 'hire' the whole environment. For a flower to blossom, you need the right soil as well as the right seed." Until the leaders in an organization realize this, they will not succeed, regardless of the talented individuals they bring into the firm. The right atmosphere allows potential leaders to bloom and grow. That is why the atmosphere needs to be valued and developed first. Even when a leader from an organization with a poor climate steals away a potential leader who is beginning to bloom from the rich "greenhouse" environment of a healthy organization, the potential leader will not continue to grow and bloom. Unless, of course, the leader has already converted the environment of his or her own organization from "arctic" to "tropical."

To see the relationship between environment and growth, look at nature. An observation was made by a man who dives for exotic fish for aquariums. According to him, one of the most popular aquarium fish is the shark. The reason for this is that sharks adapt to their environment. If you catch a small shark and confine it, it will stay a size proportionate to the aquarium in which it lives. Sharks can be six inches long and fully mature. But turn them loose in the ocean and they grow to their normal size.

The same is true of potential leaders. Some are put into an organization when they are still small, and the confining environment ensures that they stay small and underdeveloped. Only leaders can control the environment of their organization. They can be the change agents who create a climate conducive to growth.

MODEL THE DESIRED STYLE OF LEADERSHIP

Example
✗

According to noted medical missionary Albert Schweitzer, "Example is not the main thing in influencing others . . . it is the only thing." Part of creating an appealing climate is modeling leadership. People emulate what they see modeled. Positive model—positive response. Negative model—negative response. What leaders do, potential leaders around them do. What they value, their people value. The leaders' goals become their goals. Leaders set the tone. As Lee Iacocca suggests, "The speed of the boss is the speed of the team." A leader cannot demand of others what he does not demand of himself.

As you and I grow and improve as leaders, so will those we lead. We need to remember that when people follow us, they can only go as far as we go. If our growth stops, our ability to lead will stop along with it. Neither personality nor methodology can substitute for personal growth. We cannot model what we do not possess. Begin learning and growing today, and watch those around you begin to grow. As a leader, I am primarily a follower of great principles and other great leaders.

FOCUS ON THE POTENTIAL OF THE LEADER AND THE ORGANIZATION

As stated before, those who believe in our abilities do more than stimulate us. They create an atmosphere in which it becomes easier to succeed. The opposite is also true. When a leader does not believe in us, success is very difficult for us to achieve. It becomes nearly impossible. As leaders, we cannot allow this to happen to those we lead if we expect our organizations to succeed.

To ensure success, identify the potential in each future leader and cultivate it in light of the needs of the organization. It produces a win-win situation. The mentoring leader wins because of the rising star working beneath him or her who can perform and produce. The organization wins because its mission is being fulfilled. The potential leader wins because he is being developed and improved. His future looks bright.

One of the best applications of this idea is expressed in what I call the 101 percent principle: *Find the one thing that you believe is the potential leader's greatest asset, and then give 101 percent encouragement in that area.* Focusing on a person's strengths promotes positive growth, confidence, and success as a potential leader.

FOCUS ON THE POTENTIAL LEADER'S NEEDS (DESIRES)

People often associate great achievement with a number of things: luck, timing, circumstance, or natural talent. The secret to a person's success often appears to be an elusive quality. The University of Chicago did a five-year study of leading artists, athletes, and scholars to determine what made them successful. Conducted by Dr. Benjamin Bloom, the research was based on anonymous interviews with the top twenty performers in various fields. Included were a variety of professionals such as concert pianists, Olympic swimmers, tennis players, sculptors, mathematicians, and neurologists. Bloom and his team of researchers probed for clues as to how these high achievers developed. For a more complete picture, they also interviewed their families and teachers. The report stated conclusively that drive, determination, and desire, not great natural talent, led to the extraordinary success of these individuals.

Great leaders know the desires of the people they lead. As much as potential leaders respect the knowledge and ability of their leaders, these are secondary matters to them. They don't care how much their leaders *know* until they know how much their leaders *care* . . . about their needs, their dreams, their desires. Once a leader is genuinely interested in the well-being of those around him, the determination and drive of the people in that group are activated in a remarkable way. The starting point of all achievement is drive, determination, and desire.

> **It takes a leader with vision to see the future leader within the person.**

Napoleon Bonaparte is known as one of history's greatest leaders. One of his leadership secrets was knowing the needs of his men. He first determined what his men wanted most. Then he did everything possible to help them get it. He knew this was a key to successful motivation. Most leaders do the opposite. They first decide what *they* want. Then they try to persuade others to want the same thing as much as they do.

LOOK FOR THE LEADER WITHIN THE PERSON

There is no future in any job. The future lies in the person who holds the job. It takes a leader with vision to see the future leader within the person. Michelangelo, when questioned about his masterpiece *David*, answered that the sculpture had always existed within the stone. He had simply chiseled away the rock around it. Leaders must have the same kind of vision when viewing potential leaders. Some of the qualities to look for in a person include the following:

Positiveness:	the ability to work with and see people and situations in a positive way
Servanthood:	the willingness to submit, play team ball, and follow the leader
Growth potential:	a hunger for personal growth and development; the ability to keep growing as the job expands
Follow-through:	the determination to get the job done completely and with consistency
Loyalty:	the willingness to always put the leader and the organization above personal desires
Resiliency:	the ability to bounce back when problems arise
Integrity:	trustworthiness and solid character; consistent words and walk
"Big picture" mind-set:	the ability to see the whole organization and all of its needs
Discipline:	the willingness to do what is required regardless of personal mood
Gratitude:	an attitude of thankfulness that becomes a way of life

When searching for these traits within a person, the leader should emulate gold prospectors. They are always on the lookout for potential gold mines. Every mountain is a possible opportunity to strike it rich. When they find traces of ore, they assume there is a vein and begin digging. The same is true in every organization. If you as a leader look for and find traces of gold in your people, start digging. You will uncover the mother lode!

PLACE AN EMPHASIS ON PRODUCTION, NOT POSITION AND TITLE

Organizations that place great emphasis on titles and position are teaching their employees to do the same. Employees in that type of environment can often become preoccupied with moving up the ladder to the next position or with receiving a more important-sounding title. When it comes down to it, titles are worth little. A lofty title doesn't help a poor producer. A lowly title doesn't hinder a super producer. Position, like a title, doesn't make a leader either.

In *Developing the Leader Within You*, I describe the five levels of leadership: position, permission, production, personnel development, and personhood. *Position* is the lowest level. A person who stands on his position will never have influence beyond his or her job description.

Seniority also provides little in and of itself. A survey was conducted by Accountemps, a temporary personnel service and placement organization. Executives and personnel directors were asked for the most influential factors in evaluating an employee for promotion. The results: 66 percent named specific accomplishments, 47 percent named general work habits and performance, and only 4 percent cited seniority as being important. Time on the job is no substitute for production in the job.

In an organization emphasizing production, attention and energy are devoted to doing the job and doing it well. There is a team atmosphere, with accomplishing the mission of the organization as the goal. That is the kind of climate where leaders emerge. As Charles Wilson, the former president of General Electric, said, "No matter what size the bottle, the cream always came to the top."

PROVIDE GROWTH OPPORTUNITIES

There is a story of a tourist who paused for a rest in a small town in the mountains. He went over to an old man sitting on a bench in front of the only store in town and inquired, "Friend, can you tell me something this town is noted for?" "Well," replied the old man, "I don't rightly know except that it's the starting point to the world. You can start here and go anywhere you want."

All people do not view their current location as the starting point to wherever they want to go in the world. We as leaders must encourage those around us to see themselves in such a place. Creating an environment for personal growth is critical. However, if the people around you are unaware they are in such an environment, they may not take advantage of it. That is one reason why it is important to *create opportunities for growth*. Another reason is that established leaders are in a position to know what opportunities a potential leader needs.

In order to create the right opportunities, we must look at the potential leaders around us and ask, "What does this person need in order to grow?" A generic formula will not work. If we don't fit the opportunity to the potential leader, we may find ourselves in the position of offering things that our people don't need.

Ernest Campbell, a faculty member at Union Theological Seminary, tells an enlightening story:

> A woman went to a pet store and purchased a parrot to keep her company. She took her new pet home but returned the next day to report, "That parrot hasn't said a word yet!"

"Does it have a mirror?" asked the storekeeper. "Parrots like to be able to look at themselves in the mirror." So she bought the mirror and returned home.

The next day she was back, announcing that the bird still wasn't speaking.

"What about a ladder?" the storekeeper said. "Parrots enjoy walking up and down a ladder." So she bought a ladder and returned home.

Sure enough, the next day she was back with the same story—still no talk.

"Does the parrot have a swing? Birds enjoy relaxing on a swing." She bought the swing and went home.

The next day she returned to the store to announce the bird had died.

"I'm terribly sorry to hear that," said the storekeeper. "Did the bird ever say anything before it died?"

"Yes," the lady replied. "It said, 'Don't they sell any food down there?'"

Many leaders are like the lady in the story. They want their people to produce. When the people don't, the leaders provide them with all the things some expert says they are supposed to like. However, the leaders themselves never look at their people to see what they really need.

As you examine potential leaders and determine what each needs, keep in mind these ideas for growth opportunities:

- Expose the potential leader to people successful in his field.

- Provide a secure environment where the potential leader is free to take risks.

• Provide the potential leader with an experienced mentor.

• Provide the potential leader with the tools and resources she needs.

• Spend the time and money to train the potential leader in his areas of need.

The idea of building potential leaders through growth opportunities can be summed up in this poem by Edwin Markham:

We are blind until we see
That in the human plan
Nothing is worth the making
If it does not make the man.

Why build these cities glorious
If man unbuilded goes?
In vain we build the world
Unless the builder also grows.[1]

LEAD (DON'T MANAGE) WITH VISION

An important part of leadership involves casting vision. Some leaders forget to cast vision because they get caught up in managing. True leaders recognize a difference between leaders and managers. Managers are maintainers, tending to rely on systems and controls. Leaders are innovators and creators who rely on people. Creative ideas become reality when people who are in a position to act catch the vision of their innovative leader.

An effective vision provides guidance. It gives direction for an organization . . . direction that cannot effectively result from rules and regulations, policy manuals, or organizational charts. True direction for an organization is born with a vision. It begins when the leader accepts it. It gains acceptance when the leader models it. And it becomes reality when the people respond to it.

Do Big Things

Nearly everything a leader does hinges on the type of vision he has. If his vision is small, so will be his results and his followers. A high-ranking French official who understood this concept once expressed it thus when addressing Winston Churchill: "If you are doing big things, you attract big men. If you are doing little things, you attract little men. Little men usually cause trouble." An effective vision attracts winners.

Too often people limit their own potential. They think small. They are afraid of risk. People no longer willing to stretch are no longer able to grow. As author Henry Drummond says, "Unless a man undertakes more than he possibly can do, he will never do all he can do."

Spend More Effort on the "Farm Team" Than on the Free Agents

Once a leader has a vision, he needs to build a team to carry it out. Where does he find winners? It's not easy. In fact, most winners are made, not found. In major league baseball, teams generally recruit players in one of two ways. They either bring players up from their own minor league farm teams or go outside the organization in search of free agents. Time after time, baseball fans have seen their teams bring in expensive free agents with the expectation of winning a World Series. Time after time they are disappointed.

The "farm team" method involves bringing in the best undeveloped players who can be found and allowing them to start with the organization at their own level. They are coached and developed. Their managers and coaches discover their strengths and weaknesses and find the right positions for them. The players gain experience and have an opportunity to bring up their level of play. If their performance is good enough, they get promoted to the major league team.

The vast majority of the leadership in our organization is recruited and promoted from within. It has not always been easy, but there are tremendous advantages in using the farm-team method. The first is that you already know the individual's character and attitude. When you interview somebody on the outside, you take a risk. You have to base a hiring decision on what the potential employee and the recommendations tell you. Job descriptions on a resume address skills, not character. Most employers agree that character and attitude are the most important factors in hiring a new employee. Skills can be taught.

The second advantage is that a person promoted from within already knows the organization and its people. A successful employee who is considered for promotion has already caught the leader's vision. He shares the philosophy of the organization. He has spent time building relationships with the people. A person brought in from outside must spend time learning these things. Once hired, he may even be unwilling or unable to assimilate. When you hire people from within, they hit the ground running.

The third advantage is that a person brought up from the farm team is a proven performer. You have already seen his gifts and impact. You know he can hit the ball in your park. As a result, the risk is relatively small. With a free agent, you have had limited opportunity to observe him firsthand. It is possible that he may not be able to hit the ball in your park, because the conditions are different. Developing the talent on your farm team will require strategic action and a particular attitude from the team's leader. The leader must:

- Invest time and money in his potential leaders.

- Commit to promoting from within.

- Show his people that personal and professional growth within the organization are not only possible but also actual.

MAKE DIFFICULT DECISIONS

Willard C. Butch, chairman of the Chase Manhattan Corporation, was once given some advice by Marion Folsom, then a top Eastman Kodak Company executive: "Bill, you're going to find that 95 percent of all the decisions you'll ever make in your career could be made as well by a reasonably intelligent high school sophomore. But they'll pay you for the other five percent."

Some of the toughest decisions a leader faces concern poor performers. Great leaders make smart choices concerning them. A leader who does not effectively handle them will hurt:

- the organization's ability to achieve its purpose

- the morale of top performers

- his own credibility

- the low performers' self-image and potential effectiveness

To discover the proper course concerning a poor performer, a leader needs to ask himself, "Should this person be trained, transferred, or terminated?" The answer will determine the appropriate course of action.

If low performance is due to poor or undeveloped skills, it calls for training. Likewise, training can often benefit an employee needing to be taught the organization's philosophy or vision. Training is often the most positive of solutions, because it invests in the employee. It is also more economical to improve a current employee than start a new person from scratch.

Sometimes an employee is a low performer because he is expected to perform a job that does not match his gifts and abilities. If the employee has a good attitude and a desire to succeed, he can be transferred to a position matching his gifts. There he may flourish.

Terminating an employee is by far the most difficult of the tough decisions a leader faces. It is also one of the most important decisions he may make. In fact, removing poor performers from an organization is as important as finding good ones. Terminating a poor performer benefits the organization and everyone in it. It also gives the former employee the opportunity to reevaluate his or her potential and find the place and position where he or she can be a winner.

PAY THE PRICE THAT ATTRACTS LEADERS

Success always comes at a price. That is a lesson I learned a long time ago. My father taught me that a person can pay now and play later, or he can play now and pay later. Either way, he is going to pay.

Creating a climate for potential leaders also requires a leader to pay a price. It begins with personal growth. The leader must examine himself, ask himself the hard questions, and then determine to do the right thing regardless of atmosphere or mood. There are few ideal and leisurely settings for the disciplines of growth. Most of the significant things done in the world were done by persons who were either too busy or too sick to do them. Emotion-based companies allow the atmosphere to determine the action. Character-based companies allow the action to determine the atmosphere.

> A person can pay now and play later, or he can play now and pay later.

Successful leaders recognize that personal growth and the development of leadership skills are lifetime pursuits. Warren Bennis and Burt Nanus, in *Leaders: The Strategies for Taking Charge*, did a study of ninety top leaders in all fields. They found that "it is the capacity to develop and improve their skills that distinguishes leaders from their followers." They came to the conclusion that "leaders are perpetual learners."

Commitment to provide a climate where potential leaders may grow must start with the leader's commitment to personal growth. Answer the following questions to determine your current commitment level.

QUESTIONS ON COMMITMENT TO PERSONAL GROWTH

1. Do I have a game plan for personal growth?

Yes   No

2. Am I the leader of that plan?

Yes   No

3. Am I willing to change to keep growing, even if it means giving up my current position, if I am not experiencing growth?

Yes   No

4. Is my life an example for others to follow?:

Yes   No

5. Am I willing to pay the price to become a great leader?

Yes   No

A no on any of these questions should cause a leader to examine his plan and commitment to personal growth. A lack of commitment on the part of a leader makes it difficult for potential leaders around him to be developed. If you as a leader have not made this commitment, your future is limited, and you will never become a great leader. Now is the time to change.

The environment in which you work will influence you and those you lead. Answer the following questions to help determine your organization's dedication to developing leaders and providing a climate that promotes organizational and personal growth.

QUESTIONS TO ASK CONCERNING ORGANIZATIONAL GROWTH

1. Has the organization made a specific commitment to grow and develop people?

Seldom   Sometimes   Usually

2. Is the organization willing to spend money to develop employees' growth?

Seldom   Sometimes   Usually

3. Is the organization willing to make changes to keep itself and its people growing?

Seldom   Sometimes   Usually

4. Does the organization support leaders willing to make the difficult decisions necessary for people's personal growth and the growth of the organization?

       Seldom   Sometimes   Usually

5. Does the organization place an emphasis on production rather than position or title?

       Seldom   Sometimes   Usually

6. Does the organization provide growth opportunities for its people?

       Seldom   Sometimes   Usually

7. Do organizational leaders have vision and share it with their people?

       Seldom   Sometimes   Usually

8. Does the organization think big?

       Seldom   Sometimes   Usually

9. Does the organization promote from within?

       Seldom   Sometimes   Usually

10. Are there other leaders in the organization willing to pay the price of personal sacrifice to ensure their growth and the growth of others?

       Seldom   Sometimes   Usually

If the majority of the answers to these questions is Seldom or Sometimes, a change is in order. If the organization is controlled by you, begin changing now. If you head a department in the organization, then you are in a position to make positive changes. Do as many things as your organization will allow to create a positive climate for potential leaders. If you are in a position only to make changes for yourself, try to find someone in the organization who will develop you—or change your job. Great leaders share themselves and what they have learned with the learners who will become tomorrow's leaders. A person can impress potential leaders from a distance, but only from up close can he impact them.

Here are a few closing thoughts on creating a climate for potential leaders. Sports records provide tangible evidence of the positive changes that can occur when the right climate has been established. One Olympic athlete, Parry O'Brien, won a gold medal at

> **Great leaders share themselves and what they have learned.**

the 1952 Olympics by throwing a 16-pound shot 57 feet. In 1953 he set a new world record by throwing the shot 59 feet, 3/4 inch. Experts at the time said O'Brien, the best in the world, might beat his record by a few inches if he practiced, but they were certain that no one would ever be able to break the 60-foot barrier.

Luckily, O'Brien didn't think like an expert. As an athlete he was determined to continue improving himself. He began experimenting with different styles and invented a new technique for his event, which would become the universal style of putting the shot until the mid-1970s.

In 1956 O'Brien won at the Olympics again—not by a few inches, but by a few *feet*. He also broke the unbreakable barrier by tossing the shot 60 feet, 11 inches. O'Brien set his final record in 1959 when he threw the shot 63 feet, 4 inches. From that time on, every competitive shot-putter has tossed the shot beyond that length. Today, the record is over 75 feet.

The same is true of the four-minute mile. No one, the experts said, would ever be able to run the mile in less than four minutes. Then, in 1954, a young medical student named Roger Bannister did the impossible by breaking that barrier. Today, every world-class runner can run the mile in less than four minutes. Why? Because one man decided to keep improving. One man decided to pay the price of personal growth. He was willing to lead. As a result, he created a climate for those achievers who followed him. Are you the type of leader who is willing to pay the price and create a climate in which your people can follow you and emerge as the leaders of tomorrow?

THREE

THE LEADER'S PRIMARY RESPONSIBILITY:
IDENTIFYING POTENTIAL LEADERS

There is something much more important and scarce than ability: It is the ability to recognize ability. One of the primary responsibilities of a successful leader is to identify potential leaders. It's not always an easy job, but it is critical.

Andrew Carnegie was a master at identifying potential leaders. Once asked by a reporter how he had managed to hire forty-three millionaires, Carnegie responded that the men had not been millionaires when they started working for him. They had become millionaires as a result. The reporter next wanted to know how he had developed these men to become such valuable leaders. Carnegie replied, "Men are developed the same way gold is mined. Several tons of dirt must be moved to get an ounce of gold. But you don't go into the mine looking for dirt," he added. "You go in looking for the gold." That's exactly the way to develop positive, successful people. Look for the gold, not the dirt; the good, not the bad. The more positive qualities you look for, the more you are going to find.

> To develop positive, successful people, look for the gold, not the dirt.

SELECTING THE RIGHT PLAYERS

Professional sports organizations recognize the importance of selecting the right players. Every year, coaches and owners of professional baseball, basketball, and football teams look forward to the draft. To prepare for it, sports franchises spend much time and energy scouting new prospects. For instance, scouts from pro football organizations travel to regular-season college games, bowl games, senior-only bowl games, and camps to gain knowledge about prospective players. All of this enables the scouts to bring plenty of information back to the owners and head coaches so that when draft day arrives, the teams can pick the most promising players. Team owners and coaches know that the future success of their teams depends largely on their ability to draft effectively.

It's no different in business. You must select the right players in your organization. If you select well, the benefits are multiplied and seem nearly endless. If you select poorly, the problems are multiplied and seem endless.

Too often, leaders hire employees haphazardly. Because of desperation, lack of time, or just plain ignorance, they quickly grab any candidate who comes along. Then they hold their breath and hope everything works out. But hiring needs to be done strategically. Before you hire a new employee, your options are nearly limitless. Once you have made the hiring decision, your options are few. Hiring an employee is like skydiving: once you've jumped out of the plane, you're committed.

> Hiring an employee is like skydiving: once you've jumped out of the plane, you're committed.

The key to making the right choice depends on two things: (1) your ability to see the big picture, and (2) your ability to judge potential employees during the selection process.

It is a good idea to start with an inventory. I use this one because I always want to look inside as well as outside the organization to find candidates. I call this list the Five A's:

Assessment of needs:	What is needed?
Assets on hand:	Who are the people already in the organization who are available?
Ability of candidates:	Who is able?
Attitude of candidates:	Who is willing?
Accomplishments of candidates:	Who gets things done?

Notice that the inventory begins with an assessment of needs. The leader of the organization must base that assessment on the big picture. While he was manager of the Chicago Cubs, Charlie Grimm reportedly received a phone call from one of his scouts. The man was excited and began to shout over the telephone, "Charlie, I've landed the greatest young pitcher in the land! He struck out every man who came to bat. Twenty-seven in a row. Nobody even hit a foul until the ninth inning. The pitcher is right here with me. What shall I do?" Charlie replied, "Sign up the guy who got the foul. We're looking for hitters." Charlie knew what the team needed.

There is one situation that supersedes a needs analysis: when a truly exceptional person is available but doesn't necessarily match the current need, do whatever you can to hire him or her anyway. In the long run, that person will positively impact the organization. You see this kind of decision-making in sports. Football coaches generally draft players to fill specific needs. If they lack a strong running back, they draft the best running back available. But sometimes they get an opportunity to draft an "impact player," a superstar who can instantly change the whole complexion of the team. Incidentally, impact players usually possess not only athletic ability but also leadership skills. Even as rookies, they have all the qualities to be team captains. When I have an opportunity to hire someone who is exceptional—a superstar—I do it. Then I find a place for him or her. Good people are hard to find, and there is always room for one more productive person in an organization.

Usually we are not judging superstars, and the decisions are harder to make. How do pro sports teams evaluate potential players? Many use a grid that yields a score for each player based on his abilities. In the same way, we need to have a tool to help evaluate people's potential as leaders. Here is a list of twenty-five characteristics to help you rate and identify a potential leader.

ASSESSMENT OF CURRENT LEADERSHIP QUALITIES (FOR POTENTIAL LEADERS)

SCALE
0=Never 1=Seldom 2=Sometimes 3=Usually 4=Always

1. The person has influence.   0 1 2 3 4

2. The person has self-discipline.   0 1 2 3 4

3. The person has a good track record.   0   1   2   3   4

4. The person has strong people skills.   0   1   2   3   4

5. The person has the ability to solve   0   1   2   3   4
   problems.

6. The person does not accept the   0   1   2   3   4
   status quo.

7. The person sees the big picture.   0   1   2   3   4

8. The person has the ability to   0   1   2   3   4
   handle stress.

9. The person displays a positive   0   1   2   3   4
   spirit.

10. The person understands people.   0   1   2   3   4

11. The person is free of personal   0   1   2   3   4
    problems.

12. The person is willing to take   0   1   2   3   4
    responsibility.

13. The person is free from anger.   0   1   2   3   4

14. The person is willing to make   0   1   2   3   4
    changes.

15. The person has integrity.   0   1   2   3   4

16. The person is growing closer   0   1   2   3   4
    to God.

17. The person has the ability to see   0   1   2   3   4
    what has to be done next.

18. The person is accepted as a   0   1   2   3   4
    leader by others.

19. The person has the ability and   0   1   2   3   4
    desire to keep learning.

20. The person has a manner that   0   1   2   3   4
    draws people.

21. The person has a good self-image.   0   1   2   3   4

22. The person has a willingness to   0   1   2   3   4
    serve others.

23. The person has the ability to   0   1   2   3   4
    bounce back when problems arise.

24. The person has the ability to   0   1   2   3   4
    develop other leaders.

25. The person takes initiative.   0   1   2   3   4

Total Points:_____

When assessing a potential leader, pay more attention to the quality of the person as addressed by the characteristics than to the specific score. Since leaders grade differently, scores vary. Here is my grading scale:

90–100   Great leader (should be mentoring other good and great leaders)

80–89   Good leader (must keep growing and keep mentoring others)

70–79   Emerging leader (focus on growth and begin mentoring others)

60–69   Bursting with potential (excellent person to be developed)

Below 60   Needs growth (may not be ready to be mentored as a leader)

The "Below 60" category is often the most difficult to judge. Some people in this group will never become leaders. Others are capable of becoming great leader. The better leader the evaluator is, the better his judgment of a person's leadership potential. Thus, it is important that a successful leader do the interviewing and hiring of potential leaders.

In *Inc.* magazine, marketing expert I. Martin Jacknis identifies a trend he has seen in hiring. He terms it the *Law of Diminishing Expertise*. Simply stated, leaders tend to hire people whose ability and expertise are beneath their own. As a result, when organizations grow and more people are hired, the number of people with low expertise far exceeds the leaders who have great expertise.

Here's how this works. Let's say, for example, you are an outstanding leader with great vision, self-discipline, right priorities, and super problem-solving skills. You score a 95 on the Assessment of Current Leadership Qualities. So you decide to start your own business, called *Leader to Leader, Inc.* Your business does so well that you soon need four new employees. You would like to hire four 95s, but, chances are, 95s want to work for themselves (just as you do) and are not available. You need help, so you hire four 85s, not as skilled as you, but each a leader in his or her own right.

I must mention at this crucial stage in the company's development, you may have been tempted to hire less than 85s for your staff. You may be thinking to yourself, *The four people I hire just have to follow me and my direction, and the company will do fine. I can settle for a couple of followers who are 65s.* That is the critical error many leaders make. By selecting followers rather than potential leaders, the leader of an organization limits its potential for growth. But for the moment, let's say that you don't make that mistake, and you hire four leaders with scores of 85.

You and your team of leaders are doing great. The business can hardly keep up with demand. Then you land a national account. Your hard work has paid off, but you now estimate that you will need about one hundred employees working around the clock to carry the load. You now need to build a whole organization.

You begin with your faithful four employees. They're good leaders, they helped you make it, and you're dedicated to promoting from within. They are going to be your four managers. You decide the best way to structure the new organization is to have one manager overseeing sales, and each of the other three managers overseeing an eight-hour shift to keep production going twenty-four hours a day. Each manager will supervise two assistant managers and about twenty other employees.

The four managers hire their assistants who, consistent with the law of diminishing expertise, rate as 75s. The managers give the assistants the job of hiring the twenty employees. You guessed it. They hire 65s. As a result, almost overnight, the company whose staff leadership score averaged 87 and looked like this:

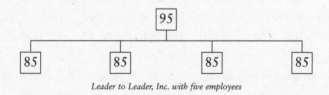

Leader to Leader, Inc. with five employees

now has a leadership score averaging 67 and looks like this:

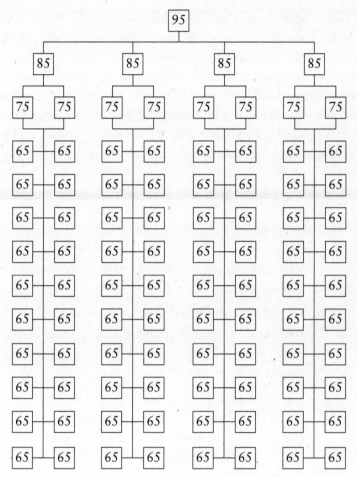

Leader to Leader, Inc. with nearly one hundred employees

The whole complexion of *Leader to Leader, Inc.* has changed. And if the original four you hired had not been leaders, you would have been in even worse trouble.

This is a slightly exaggerated example. Most companies don't go from five to one hundred employees overnight. But the organizations of great leaders expand quickly. What's important is that you can actually see the impact hiring has on an organization. In this example, what was once an organization comprised of high producers is now an organization overwhelmed with marginal producers. If the sales department lands another national account, another expansion will occur. In the next expansion, the assistant mangers, who are 75s, will probably be promoted to become new managers, and the company will take another downturn, possibly putting its average in the mediocre 50s.

Fortunately, there are ways to combat the trend toward mediocrity:

1. Make Hiring the Responsibility of a Highly Developed Leader
   Since undeveloped people hire less developed people, improve the source.

2. Hire the Most Highly Developed Leaders You Can Get
   Don't settle for poor performers. Keep in mind that one great person will always out-produce and out-perform two mediocre people.

3. Commit to Modeling Leadership
   Let all the people in the organization know what is expected of them. Many potential leaders will try to reach a standard they can see.

4. Commit to Developing Those Around You
   If you develop the potential leaders around you, by the next expansion, the dedicated assistant managers who were 75s will be 85s and ready to lead.

I would say that David Ogilvy, founder of the giant advertising agency Ogilvy and Mather, understood the law of diminishing expertise, based on the information Dennis Waitley gives about him in *The New Dynamics of Winning*. He states that Ogilvy used to give each new manager in his organization a Russian doll. The doll contained five progressively smaller dolls. A message inside the smallest one read: "If each of us hires people who are smaller than we are, we shall become a company of dwarfs. But if each of us hires people who are bigger then we are, Ogilvy and Mather will become a company of giants." Commit to finding, hiring, and developing giants.

QUALITIES TO LOOK FOR IN A LEADER

To hunt for leaders, you first need to know what they look like. Here are ten leadership qualities to seek in anyone you hire:

CHARACTER

The first thing to look for in any kind of leader or potential leader is strength of character. I have found nothing more important than this quality. Serious character flaws cannot be ignored. They will eventually make a leader ineffective—every time.

Character flaws should not be confused with weaknesses. We all have weaknesses. They can be overcome through training or experience. Character flaws cannot be changed overnight. Change usually takes a long period of time and involves significant relational investment and dedication on the part of the leader. Any person that you hire who has character flaws will be the weak link in your organization. Depending on the nature of the character flaw, the person has the potential to destroy the organization.

> **Character flaws cannot be ignored. They will eventually make a leader ineffective.**

Some of the qualities that make up good character include: honesty, integrity, self-discipline, teachability, dependability, perseverance, conscientiousness, and a strong work ethic. The words of a person with right character match the deeds. His reputation is solid. His manner is straightforward.

The assessment of character can be difficult. Warning signs to watch for include:

- a person's failure to take responsibility for his actions or circumstances

- unfulfilled promises or obligations

- failure to meet deadlines

You can tell much about a person's ability to lead others from how well he manages his own life.

Finally, look at his interactions with others. You can also tell much about a person's character from his relationships. Examine his relationships with superiors, colleagues, and subordinates. Talk to your employees to find out how the potential leader treats them. This will give you additional insight.

INFLUENCE

Leadership is influence. Every leader has these two characteristics: (A) he is going somewhere and (B) he is able to persuade others to go with him. Influence by itself is not enough. That influence must be measured to determine its *quality*. When looking at a potential employee's influence, examine the following:

What is the leader's level of influence? Does that person have followers due to position (he uses the power of his job title), permission (he has developed relationships which motivate), production (he and his followers consistently produce results), personnel development (he has developed others around him), or personhood (he transcends the organization and develops people on a world-class scale)?

Who influences the leader? Who is he following? People become like their models. Is his model ethical? Does his model have the right priorities?

Whom does he influence? Likewise, the quality of the follower will indicate the quality of the leader. Are his followers positive producers or a bunch of mediocre yes-men?

Stuart Briscoe, in *Discipleship for Ordinary People*, tells the story of a young clergyman who officiated at the funeral of a war veteran. The veteran's military friends wanted to participate in the service to honor their comrade, so they requested that the young pastor lead them down to the casket for a moment of remembrance and then out through a side door. The occasion failed to have the desired effect when the clergyman led them through the wrong door. In full view of the other mourners, the men marched with military precision into a broom closet and had to beat a hasty and confused retreat. Every leader must know where he is going. And every follower had better be sure he's behind a leader who knows what he's doing.

POSITIVE ATTITUDE

A positive attitude is one of the most valuable assets a person can have in life. My belief in this is so strong that I wrote an entire book on the subject, *The Winning Attitude: Your Key to Personal Success*. So often, what people say their problem is really isn't their problem. Their problem is the attitude which causes them to handle life's obstacles poorly.

The individual whose attitude causes him to approach life from an entirely positive perspective is someone who can be called a no-limit person. In other words, the person doesn't accept the normal limitations of life as most people do. He or she is determined to walk to the very edge of his potential, or his product's potential, before he accepts defeat. People with positive attitudes are able to go places where others can't. They do things that others can't. They are not restricted by self-imposed limitations.

A person with a positive attitude is like a bumblebee. The bumblebee should not be able to fly, because the size, weight, and shape of its body in relationship to its wingspread makes flying aerodynamically impossible. But the bumblebee, being ignorant of scientific theory, flies anyway and makes honey every day.

This no-limit mind-set allows a person to start each day with a positive disposition, as did an elevator operator I once read about. One Monday morning, in a full elevator, the man began humming a tune. One passenger, irritated by the man's mood, snapped, "What are you so happy about?" "Well, sir," replied the operator happily, "I ain't never lived this day before." Not only does the future look bright when the attitude is right, but the present is much more enjoyable too. The positive person understands that the journey is as enjoyable as the destination.

Think of the attitude like this:

> It is the advance man of our true selves.
> Its roots are inward, but its fruit is outward.
> It is our best friend or our worst enemy.
> It is more honest and more consistent than our words.
> It is an outward look based on past experiences.
> It is a thing which draws people to us or repels them.
> It is never content until it is expressed.
> It is the librarian of our past.
> It is the speaker of our present.
> It is the prophet of our future.[1]

Attitude sets the tone, not only for the leader with the attitude, but also for the people following him.

EXCELLENT PEOPLE SKILLS

A leader without people skills soon has no followers. Andrew Carnegie, a fantastic leader, is reported to have paid Charles Schwab a salary of $1 million a year simply because of his excellent people skills. Carnegie had other leaders who understood the job better and whose experience and training were better suited to the work. But they lacked the essential human quality of being able to get others to help them, and Schwab could get the best out of his fellow workers. People may admire a person who has only talent and ability, but they will not follow him—not for long.

Excellent people skills involve a genuine concern for others, the ability to understand people, and the decision to make positive inter-action with others a primary concern. Our behavior toward others determines their behavior toward us. A successful leader knows this.

EVIDENT GIFTS

Every person God creates has gifts. One of our jobs as leaders is to make an assessment of those gifts when considering a person for employment. I think of every job candidate as a "wanna be" leader. My observation is that there are four types of wanna-bes:

Never be. Some people simply lack the ability to do a particular job. As I mentioned before, all people are gifted. However, not all are gifted for the particular task at hand. A *never be* who is directed into an area where he is not gifted becomes frustrated, often blames others for his lack of success, and eventually burns out. Redirected, he has a chance of reaching his potential.

Could be. A *could be* is a person with the right gifts and abilities but lacking self-discipline. He may even be a person with superstar abilities who just can't get himself to perform. This person needs to develop the self-discipline to "just do it."

Should be. A *should be* is someone with raw talent (gifts) but few skills for harnessing that ability. He needs training. Once he is given help in developing those skills, he will begin to become the person he was created to be.

Must be. The only things a *must be* lacks is opportunity. He has the right gifts, the right skills, and the right attitude. He has the drive to be the person he was created to be. It is up to you to be the leader who gives him that opportunity. If you don't he will find someone else who will.

God creates all people with natural gifts. But he also makes them with two ends, one to sit on and one to think with. Success in life is dependent on which one of these ends is used the most, and it's a toss-up: Heads you win, and tails you lose!

PROVEN TRACK RECORD

Poet Archibald MacLeish once said, "There is only one thing more painful than learning from experience, and that is not learning from experience." Leaders who learn this truth develop successful track records over time. Everyone who breaks new ground, who strives to do something, makes mistakes. People without proven track records either haven't learned from their mistakes or haven't tried.

I've worked with many talented people who've established tremendous track records. When I first started my organization, two men in particular stood out as first-rate leaders capable of the highest quality of leadership (they score in the top category on the Assessment of Current Leadership Qualities). Dick Peterson, who worked with IBM for years, quickly demonstrated that experience had not been wasted on him. Dick already had a proven track record when I asked him to team with me in 1985 to start one of my companies, INJOY. In the beginning, we were long on potential and short on resources. Dick's hard work, planning, and insight turned a shoestring business operating out of his garage into an enterprise producing materials and influencing tens of thousands of leaders nationally and internationally every year. For fifteen years Dick served as the president of INJOY and helped get the company off the ground.

Dan Reiland has quite a different story. Dan was totally a product of the farm team. He started as a church member at Skyline—the church I led as senior pastor for fourteen years. After attending seminary, he returned to the church as an intern.

> **A proven leader always has a proven track record.**

He was not the best intern we ever had. In fact, at one point I thought he wasn't going to make it. But through his hard work and mentoring on my part, he soon became one of the finest pastors on staff and developed an outstanding track record. Because of that record I asked him to become the executive pastor of the church and continued to train him. When I left the pastorate in 1995 to lead INJOY full time, Dan came with me to serve as a vice president, and he became a nationally recognized church consultant. Recently Dan returned to full-time ministry as the executive pastor of Crossroads Community Church. And no matter where Dan is leading he excels in his ability to develop other leaders.

Management expert Robert Townsend notes, "Leaders come in all sizes, ages, shapes, and conditions. Some are poor administrators, some not overly bright. But there is one clue for spotting them. Since most people *per se* are mediocre, the true leader can be recognized because somehow or other, his people consistently turn in superior performances." Always check a candidate's past performance. A proven leader always has a proven track record.

CONFIDENCE

People will not follow a leader who does not have confidence in himself. In fact, people are naturally attracted to people who convey confidence. An excellent example can be seen in an incident in Russia during an attempted coup. Army tanks had surrounded the government building housing President Boris Yeltsin and his pro-democracy supporters. High-level military leaders had ordered the tank commander to open fire and kill Yeltsin. As the army rolled into position, Yeltsin strode from the building, climbed up on a tank, looked the commander in the eye, and thanked him for coming over to the side of democracy. Later the commander admitted that they had not intended to go over to his side. Yeltsin had appeared so confident and commanding that the soldiers talked after he left and decided to join him.

Confidence is characteristic of a positive attitude. The greatest achievers and leaders remain confident regardless of circumstances. There's a wonderful story about baseball great Ty Cobb's confidence: When Cobb was seventy years old, a reporter asked, "What do you think you'd hit if you were playing these days?" Cobb, a lifetime .367 hitter, said, "About .290, maybe .300." The reporter said, "That's because of the travel, the night games, the artificial turf, and all the new pitches like the slider, right?" "No," said Cobb, "it's because I'm seventy." Strong confident leaders recognize and appreciate confidence in others.

Reprinted with special permission of King Features Syndicate

Confidence is not simply for show. Confidence empowers. A good leader has the ability to instill within his people confidence in himself. A great leader has the ability to instill within his people confidence in themselves.

SELF-DISCIPLINE

Great leaders always have self-discipline—without exception. Unfortunately, our society seeks instant gratification rather than self-discipline. We want instant breakfast, fast food, movies on demand, and quick cash from ATMs. But success doesn't come instantly. Neither does the ability to lead. As General Dwight D. Eisenhower said, "There are no victories at bargain prices."

Because we live in a society of instant gratification, we cannot take for granted that the potential leaders we interview will have self-discipline—that they will be willing to pay the price of great leadership. When it comes to self-discipline, people choose one of two things: the pain of discipline which comes from sacrifice and growth or the pain of regret which comes from the easy road and missed opportunities. Each person in life chooses. In *Adventures in Achievement*, E. James Rohn says that the pain of discipline weighs ounces. Regret weighs tons.

There are two areas of self-discipline we must look for in potential leaders. The first is in the emotions. Effective leaders recognize that their emotional reactions are their own responsibility. A leader who decides not to allow other people's actions to dictate his reactions experiences an empowering freedom. As the Greek philosopher Epictetus said, "No person is free who is not master of himself."

> **A great leader has the ability to instill within his people confidence in themselves.**

The second area concerns time. Every person on the planet is given the same allotment of minutes in a day. But each person's level of self-discipline dictates how effectively those minutes are used. Disciplined people are always growing, always striving for improvement, and they maximize the use of their time. I have found three things that characterize disciplined leaders:

- They have identified specific long- and short-term goals for themselves.

- They have a plan for achieving those goals.

- They have a desire that motivates them to continue working to accomplish those goals.

Progress comes at a price. When you interview a potential leader, determine whether he or she is willing to pay the price. The author of the popular cartoon comic strip *Ziggy* recognized this when he drew the following scene:

As our friend Ziggy, in his little automobile, drove down a road, he saw two signs. The first stated in bold letters, THE ROAD TO SUCCESS. Farther down the road stood the second sign. It read, PREPARE TO STOP FOR TOLLS.

EFFECTIVE COMMUNICATION SKILLS

Never underestimate the importance of communication. It consumes enormous amounts of our time. One study, reported by D. K. Burlow in *The Process of Communication*, states that the average American spends 70 percent of his active hours each day communicating verbally. Without the ability to communicate, a leader cannot effectively cast his vision and call his people to act on that vision. President Gerald Ford once said, "Nothing in life is more important than the ability to communicate effectively." A leader is not capable of reaching his potential without effective communication skills.

A leader's ability to convey confidence and his ability to communicate effectively are similar. Both require action on his part and a response from the follower. Communication is positive *interaction*. When communication is one-sided, it can be comical. You may have heard the story of the frustrated judge preparing to hear a divorce case:

> **Liking people is the beginning of the ability to communicate.**

"Why do you want a divorce?" the judge asked. "On what grounds?"

"All over. We have an acre and a half," responded the woman.

"No, no," said the judge. "Do you have a grudge?"

"Yes, sir. Fits two cars."

"I need a reason for the divorce," said the judge impatiently.

"Does he beat you up?"

"Oh, no. I'm up at six every day to do my exercises. He gets up later."

"Please," said the exasperated judge. "What is the reason you want a divorce?"

"Oh," she replied. "We can't seem to communicate with each other."

When I look at a potential leader's communication skills, I look for the following.

A genuine concern for the person he's talking to. When people sense that you have a concern for them, they are willing to listen to what you have to say. Liking people is the beginning of the ability to communicate.

The ability to focus on the responder. Poor communicators are focused on themselves and their own opinions. Good communicators focus on the response of the person they're talking to. Good communicators also read body language. When I interview a potential employee, and he can't read in my body language that I'm ready to move on to another subject, it sends up a red flag.

The ability to communicate with all kinds of people. A good communicator has the ability to set a person at ease. He can find a way to relate to nearly anyone of any background.

Eye contact with the person he's speaking to. Most people who are being straight with you are willing to look you in the eye. Personal integrity and conviction make communication credible.

A warm smile. The fastest way to open the lines of communication is to smile. A smile overcomes innumerable communication barriers, crossing the boundaries of culture, race, age, class, gender, education, and economic status.

If I expect a person to lead, I must also expect him to be able to communicate.

DISCONTENT WITH THE STATUS QUO

I've told my staff before that *status quo* is Latin for "the mess we're in." Leaders see what is, but more important, they have vision for what could be. They are never content with things as they are. To be leading, by definition, is to be in front, breaking new ground, conquering new worlds, moving away from the status quo. Donna Harrison states, "Great leaders are never satisfied with current levels of performance. They constantly strive for higher and higher levels of achievement." They move beyond the status quo themselves, and they ask the same of those around them.

> **A leader who loves the status quo soon becomes a follower.**

Dissatisfaction with the status quo does not mean a negative attitude or grumbling. It has to do with willingness to be different and take risks. A person who refuses to risk change fails to grow. A leader who loves the status quo soon becomes a follower. Raymond Smith, former CEO and Chairman of the Bell Atlantic Corporation, once remarked, "Taking the safe road, doing your job, and not making any waves may not get you fired (right away, at least), but it sure won't do much for your career or your company over the long haul. We're not dumb. We know that administrators are easy to find and cheap to keep. Leaders—risk takers—are in very short supply. And ones with vision are pure gold."

Risk seems dangerous to people more comfortable with old problems than new solutions. The difference between the energy and time that it takes to put up with the old problems and the energy and time it takes to come up with new solutions is surprisingly small.

> **Seek people who seek solutions.**

The difference is attitude. When seeking potential leaders, seek people who seek solutions.

Good leaders deliberately seek out and find potential leaders. Great leaders not only find them, but also transform them into other great leaders. An ability to recognize ability and a strategy for finding leaders make it happen. What is your plan for locating and identifying potential leaders?

FOUR

THE LEADER'S CRUCIAL TASK:
NURTURING POTENTIAL LEADERS

Many organizations today fail to tap into their potential. Why? Because the only reward they give their employees is a paycheck. The relationship between employer and employee never develops beyond that point. Successful organizations take a different approach. In exchange for the work a person gives, he receives not only his paycheck, but also nurturing from the people for whom he works. And nurturing has the ability to transform people's lives.

Once you have identified potential leaders, you need to begin the work of building them into the leaders they can become. To do this you need a strategy. I use the *BEST* acronym as a reminder of what people need when they get started with my organization. They need me to:

> **B** *elieve in them.*
>
> **E** *ncourage them.*
>
> **S** *hare with them.*
>
> **T** *rust them.*

> **Nurturing has the ability to transform people's lives.**

The *BEST* technique is the beginning of the next element of developing the leaders around you: nurturing potential leaders.

Nurturing benefits everyone. Who wouldn't be more secure and motivated when his leader *believes* in him, *encourages* him, *shares* with him, and *trusts* him? People are more productive when nurtured. Even more important, nurturing creates a strong emotional and professional foundation within workers who have leadership potential. Later, using training and development, a leader can be built on that foundation.

The nurturing process involves more than just encouragement. It also includes modeling. In fact, the leader's major responsibility in the nurturing process is modeling . . . leadership, a strong work ethic, responsibility, character, openness, consistency, communication, and a belief in people. Even when he is in the process of giving to the people around him, he is also modeling. The modeling process is at its best when a leader chooses a model of his own to emulate and then becomes a model to his team members. As eighteenth-century writer Oliver Goldsmith once said, "People seldom improve when they have no other model but themselves to copy." We leaders must provide ourselves as models to copy.

Mark Twain once joked, "To do right is wonderful. To teach others to do right is even more wonderful—and much easier." I have a corollary to Twain's idea: "To lead others to do right is wonderful. To do right and then lead them is more wonderful— and harder." Like Twain, I recognize that the self-disciplines of doing right and then teaching others to do right are made difficult by human nature. Everyone can find excuses for not giving to those around them. Great leaders know the difficulties and nurture their people anyway. They know that there are people who will respond positively to what they give, and they focus on those positive results.

Here are the things I have found a leader must do to nurture the potential leaders around him.

CHOOSE A LEADERSHIP MODEL FOR YOURSELF

As leaders, you and I are first responsible for finding good models for ourselves. Give careful thought to which leaders you will follow because they will determine your course. I have developed six questions to ask myself before picking a model to follow:

DOES MY MODEL'S LIFE DESERVE A FOLLOWING?

This question relates to quality of character. If the answer is not a clear yes, I have to be very careful. I will become like the people I follow, and I don't want models with flawed character.

DOES MY MODEL'S LIFE HAVE A FOLLOWING?

This question looks at credibility. It is possible to be the very first person to discover a leader worth following, but it doesn't happen very often. If the person has no following, he or she may not be worth following.

If my answer to either of the first two questions is no, I don't have to bother with the other four. I need to look for another model.

WHAT IS THE MAIN STRENGTH THAT INFLUENCES OTHERS TO FOLLOW MY MODEL?

What does the model have to offer me? What is his best? Also note that strong leaders have weaknesses as well as strengths. I don't want to inadvertently emulate the weaknesses.

DOES MY MODEL PRODUCE OTHER LEADERS?

The answer to this question will tell me whether the model's leadership priorities match mine in regard to developing new leaders.

IS MY MODEL'S STRENGTH REPRODUCIBLE IN MY LIFE?

If I can't reproduce his strength in my life, his modeling will not benefit me. For instance, if you admire Shaquille O'Neil's ability as a basketball center, but you're only 5 feet, 9 inches tall and weigh 170 pounds, you are not going to be able to reproduce his strengths. Find appropriate models . . . but strive for improvement. Don't be too quick to say that a strength is not reproducible. Most are. Don't limit your potential.

IF MY MODEL'S STRENGTH IS REPRODUCIBLE IN MY LIFE, WHAT STEPS MUST I TAKE TO DEVELOP AND DEMONSTRATE THAT STRENGTH?

You must develop a plan of action. If you only answer the questions and never implement a plan to develop those strengths in yourself, you are only performing an intellectual exercise.

The models we choose may or may not be accessible to us in a personal way. Some may be national figures, such as a president. Or they may be people from history. They can certainly benefit you, but not the way a personal mentor can.

GUIDELINES FOR MENTORING RELATIONSHIPS

When you find someone who can personally mentor you, use these guidelines to help develop a positive mentoring relationship with that person:

Ask the Right Questions

Give thought to questions you will ask before you meet with your mentor. Make them strategic for your own growth.

Clarify Your Level of Expectations

Generally, the goal of mentoring is improvement, not perfection. Perhaps only a few people can be truly excellent—but all of us can become better.

Accept a Subordinate, Learning Position

Don't let ego get in the way of learning. Trying to impress the mentor with your knowledge or ability will set up a mental barrier between you. It will prevent you from receiving what he is giving.

Respect the Mentor, But Don't Idolize Him

Respect allows us to accept what the mentor is teaching. But making the mentor an idol removes the ability to be objective and critical—faculties we need for adapting a mentor's knowledge and experience to ourselves.

Immediately Put into Effect What You Are Learning

In the best mentoring relationships, what is learned comes quickly into focus. Learn, practice, and assimilate.

Be Disciplined in Relating to the Mentor

Arrange for ample and consistent time, select the subject matter in advance, and do your homework to make the sessions profitable.

Reward Your Mentor with Your Own Progress

If you show appreciation but make no progress, the mentor experiences failure. Your progress is his highest reward. Strive for growth, then communicate your progress.

Don't Threaten to Give Up

Let your mentor know you have made a decision for progress and that you are a persistent person—a determined winner. Then he will know he is not wasting his time.

There is no substitute for your own personal growth. If you are not receiving and growing, you will not be able to give to the people you nurture and develop.

BUILD TRUST

I have learned that trust is the single most important factor in building personal and professional relationships. Warren Bennis and Burt Nanus call trust "the glue that binds followers and leaders together." Trust implies accountability, predictability, and reliability. More than anything else, followers want to believe in and trust their leaders. They want to be able to say, "Someday I want to be like him or her." If they don't trust you, they cannot say it. People first must believe in you before they will follow your leadership.

Trust must be built day by day. It calls for consistency. Some of the ways a leader can betray trust include: breaking promises, gossiping, withholding information, and being two-faced. These actions destroy the environment of trust necessary for the growth of potential leaders. And when a leader breaks trust, he must work twice as hard to regain it. As Christian leader Cheryl Biehl once said, "One of the realities of life is that if you can't trust a person at all points, you can't truly trust him or her at any point."

Every fall I look forward to seeing poor Charlie Brown try to placekick a football. He always ends up on his face or back because Lucy, his holder, jerks the ball away at the last moment. After she pulls the ball away, Lucy often tells Charlie she is trying to teach him not to be so trusting. But he keeps on trying to kick the football anyway, year after year. Why? Charlie really does want to trust people. Lucy is not a leader, and she never will be. Leadership can only function on the basis of trust; Lucy is untrustworthy.

> **Leadership can only function on the basis of trust.**

People will not follow a leader they do not trust. It is the leader's responsibility to actively develop that trust in him from the people around him. Trust is built on many things:

T *ime.*   Take time to listen and give feedback on performance.

R *espect.*   Give the potential leader respect and he will return it with trust.

U *nconditional Positive Regard.*   Show acceptance of the person.

S *ensitivity.*   Anticipate the feelings and needs of the potential leader.

T *ouch.*   Give encouragement—a handshake, high five, or pat on the back.

Once people trust their leader as a person, they become able to trust his leadership.

SHOW TRANSPARENCY

All leaders make mistakes. They are a part of life. Successful leaders recognize their errors, learn from them, and work to correct their faults. A study of 105 executives determined many of the characteristics shared by successful executives. One particular trait was identified as the most valuable: They admitted their mistakes and accepted the consequences rather than trying to blame others.

We live among people who try to make someone else responsible for their actions or circumstances. People don't want to reap the consequences of their actions. You can see this attitude everywhere. Television advertisements invite us daily to sue "even if you were at fault in an accident" or "declare bankruptcy" to avoid creditors. A leader who is willing to take responsibility for his actions and be honest and transparent with his people is someone they will admire, respect, and trust. That leader is also someone they can learn from.

OFFER TIME

People cannot be nurtured from a distance or by infrequent, short spurts of attention. They need you to spend time with them—planned time, not just a few words on the way to a meeting. I make it a priority to stay in touch with the leaders in my organization. I plan and perform training sessions for my staff, I schedule one-on-one time for mentoring, and I schedule meetings where team members can share information. Often I'll take a potential leader to lunch. I frequently check with my people to see how their area of responsibility is progressing and give assistance if needed.

> **Time spent with a potential leader is an investment.**

We live in a fast-paced, demanding world, and time is a difficult thing to give. It is a leader's most valuable commodity. Peter Drucker wrote, "Nothing else, perhaps, distinguishes effective executives as much as their tender loving care of time." Time is valuable, but time spent with a potential leader is an investment. When you give of yourself, it benefits you, the organization, and the receiver. Nurtur-ing leaders must maintain a giving attitude. Norman Vincent Peale expressed it well when he said that the man who lives for himself is a failure; the man who lives for others has achieved true success.

BELIEVE IN PEOPLE

When you believe in people, you motivate them and release their potential. And people can sense intuitively when a person really believes in them. Anyone can see people as they are. It takes a leader to see what they can become, encourage them to grow in that direction, and believe that they will do it. People always grow toward a leader's expectations, not his criticism and examinations. Examinations merely *gauge* progress. Expectations *promote* progress. You can hire people to work for you, but you must win their hearts by believing in them in order to have them work with you.

> **When you believe in people, you motivate them and release their potential.**

GIVE ENCOURAGEMENT

Too many leaders expect their people to encourage themselves. But most people require outside encouragement to propel them forward. It is vital to their growth. Physician George Adams found encouragement to be so vital to a person's existence that he called it "oxygen to the soul."

New leaders need to be encouraged. When they arrive in a new situation, they encounter many changes and undergo many changes themselves. Encouragement helps them reach their potential; it empowers them by giving them energy to continue when they make mistakes.

Use lots of positive reinforcement with your people. Don't take acceptable work for granted; thank people for it. Praise a person every time you see improvement. And personalize your encouragement any time you can. Remember, what motivates one person may leave another cold or even irritated. Find out what works with each of your people and use it.

UCLA basketball coach John Wooden told players who scored to give a smile, wink, or nod to the player who gave them a good pass. "What if he's not looking?" asked a team member. Wooden replied, "I guarantee he'll look." Everyone values encouragement and looks for it—especially when his leader is a consistent encourager.

EXHIBIT CONSISTENCY

Consistency is a crucial part of nurturing potential leaders, just as it is in any other kind of nurturing. When we are consistent, our people learn to trust us. They are able to grow and develop because they know what to expect from us. They can answer the question, "What would my leader do in this situation?" when they face difficult decisions. They become secure because they know what our response to them will be, regardless of circumstances.

Perhaps you've heard the story about the farmer who had experienced several bad years. He went to see the manager of his bank:

"I've got some good news and some bad news to tell you. Which would you like to hear first?" the farmer asked.

"Why don't you tell me the bad news first and get it over with?" the banker replied.

"Okay. With the bad drought and inflation and all, I won't be able to pay anything on my mortgage this year, either on the principal or the interest."

"Well, that is pretty bad."

"It gets worse. I also won't be able to pay anything on the loan for all that machinery I bought, not on the principal or interest."

"Wow, is that ever bad!"

"It's worse than that. You remember I also borrowed to buy seed and fertilizer and other supplies. Well, I can't pay anything on that either—principal or interest."

"That's awful and that's enough! Tell me what the good news is."

"The good news," replied the farmer with a smile, "is that I intend to keep on doing business with you."[1]

Fortunately, most of our potential leaders do better than our friend the farmer. Unlike him, they won't need consistent support for quite so long before they are able to turn things around. When we believe in our potential leaders, and we consistently support and encourage them, we give them the added strength they need to hang in there and perform well for us.

HOLD HOPE HIGH

Hope is one of the greatest gifts leaders can give to those around them. Its power should never be underestimated. It takes a great leader to give hope to people when they can't find it within themselves. Winston Churchill recognized the value of hope. He was prime minister of England during some of the darkest hours of World War II.

He was once asked by a reporter what his country's greatest weapon had been against Hitler's Nazi regime. Without pausing for a moment he said: "It was what England's greatest weapon has always been— hope."

> **It is the leader's job to hold hope high.**

People will continue working, struggling, and trying if they have hope. Hope lifts morale. It improves self-image. It reenergizes people. It raises their expectations. It is the leader's job to hold hope high, to instill it in the people he leads. Our people will have hope only if we give it to them. And we will have hope to give if we maintain the right attitude. Clare Boothe Luce, in *Europe in the Spring*, quotes Battle of Verdun hero Marshal Foch as saying, "There are no hopeless situations: there are only men who have grown hopeless about them."

Maintaining hope comes from seeing the potential in every situation and staying positive despite circumstances. Dr. G. Campbell Morgan tells the story of a man whose shop burned to the ground in the great Chicago fire. He arrived at the ruins the next morning carrying a table and set it up amid the charred debris. Above the table he placed this optimistic sign: "Everything lost except wife, children, and hope. Business will resume as usual tomorrow morning."

ADD SIGNIFICANCE

No one wants to spend his time doing work that is unimportant. People want to do work that matters. Workers often say things like, "I want to feel that I've achieved, that I've accomplished, that I've made a difference. I want excellence. I want what I do to be important work. I want to make an impact." People want significance.

It is the leader's job to add significance to the lives of the people he leads: One of the ways we can do this is to make them a part of something worthwhile. Too many people simply fall into a comfortable niche in life and stay there rather than pursue goals of significance. Leaders can't afford to do that. Every leader must ask himself, "Do I want survival, success, or significance?" The best leaders desire significance and expend their time and energy in pursuit of their dreams. As former *Washington Post* CEO Katharine Graham said, "To love what you do and feel that it matters—how could anything be more fun?"

Moishe Rosen teaches a one-sentence mental exercise that is an effective tool in helping a person identify his dream. He asks a person to fill in the blanks:

If I had _____

I would _____

The idea is that if you had anything you wanted—unlimited time, unlimited money, unlimited information, unlimited staff (all the resources you could ask for)—what would you do? Your answer to that question is your dream.

Acting on your dream adds significance to your life. There is a classic example of this from history. Everyone has heard the story of Isaac Newton's discovery of the law of gravity after observing the fall of an apple. What few people know is that Edmund Halley, the astronomer who discovered Halley's Comet, is almost single-handedly responsible for Newton's theories becoming known. Halley challenged Newton to think through his original notions. He corrected Newton's mathematical errors and prepared geometrical figures to support his work. Not only did he encourage Newton to write his great work, *Mathematical Principles of Natural Philosophy*, but he edited the work, supervised its publication, and financed its printing, even though Newton was wealthier and could easily afford the printing costs.

Halley encouraged Newton to act on his dream, and it added immeasurable significance to Newton's life. Newton began to reap the rewards of prominence almost immediately. Halley received little credit, but he must have gained great satisfaction in knowing he had inspired revolutionary ideas in the advancement of scientific thought.

Identify and pursue your dream. Make it personal, attainable, measurable, visible, and expandable. The desire for significance can stretch us to our very best. And being a part of the achievement of our dream can enrich the lives of those around us.

Another way to add significance to the lives of the people you lead is to show them the big picture and let them know how they contribute to it. Many people get so caught up in the task of the moment that they cannot see the importance of what they do.

A member of my staff who was once dean of a vocational college told me about a day he was showing around a new employee. As he introduced each person and described each person's position, the receptionist overheard him say that hers was a very important position. The receptionist commented, "I'm not important. The most important thing I do each day is fill out a report."

"Without you," the dean replied, "this school wouldn't exist. Every new student who comes here talks to you first. If they don't like you, they won't like the school. If they don't like the school, they won't come to school here, and we would soon run out of students. We would have to close our doors."

"Wow! I never thought of it that way," she replied. The dean immediately saw her appear more confident, and she sat up taller behind her desk as she answered the phone. The leader of her department had never explained to her the significance of her job. He had never explained her value to the organization. By seeing the big picture, she had significance added to her life.

PROVIDE SECURITY

Norman Cousins said, "People are never more insecure than when they become obsessed with their fears at the expense of their dreams." People who focus on their fears don't grow. They become paralyzed. Leaders are in a position to provide followers with an environment of security in which they can grow and develop. A potential leader who feels secure is more likely to take risks, try to excel, break new ground, and succeed. Great leaders make their followers feel bigger than they are. Soon the followers begin to think, act, and produce bigger than they are. Finally, they become what they think they are.

Henry Ford once said, "One of the great discoveries a man makes, one of his great surprises, is to find he can do what he was afraid he couldn't do." A nurturing leader provides the security a potential leader needs to make that discovery.

REWARD PRODUCTION

People rise to our level of expectations. They try to give us what we reward. If you want your people to produce, then you must reward production.

Thomas J. Watson, Sr., the founder of IBM, was famous for carrying a checkbook as he walked through offices and plants. Whenever he saw somebody doing an exceptional job, he wrote out a check to that person. It may have been for $5, $10, or $25. The amounts were small, but the impact of his action was tremendous. In many cases, people never cashed the checks. They framed them and put them on their walls. They found their reward not in the money, but in the personal recognition of their production. That's what gives significance and leads a person to give his personal best.

Even a person who is industrious and hardworking will finally get demoralized if production is discouraged rather than rewarded. You probably remember the children's story of the little red hen, the one who wanted help baking bread. Here is a modern version:

> Once upon a time there was a little red hen who scratched about the barnyard until she uncovered some grains of wheat. She called her neighbors and said, "If we plant this wheat, we shall have bread to eat. Who will help me plant it?"
>
> "Not I," said the cow.
>
> "Not I," said the duck.
>
> "Not I," said the pig.
>
> "Not I," said the goose.
>
> "Then I will," said the little red hen, and she did. The wheat grew tall and ripened into golden grain. "Who will help me reap my wheat?" asked the little red hen.
>
> "Not I," said the duck.
>
> "That's out of my classification," said the pig.
>
> "I'd lose my seniority," said the cow.
>
> "I'd lose my unemployment compensation," said the goose.
>
> "Then I will," said the little red hen, and she did.
>
> At last, it came time to bake the bread. "Who will help me bake the bread?" asked the little red hen.
>
> "That would be overtime for me," said the cow.
>
> "I'd lose my welfare benefits," said the duck.
>
> "If I'm to be the only helper, that would be discrimination," said the goose.

"Then I will," said the little red hen. She baked five loaves and held them up for her neighbors to see. They all wanted some. In fact, they demanded a share. But the little red hen said, "No, I can eat the five loaves myself."

"Excess profits!" yelled the cow.

"Capitalist leech!" cried the duck.

"I demand equal rights!" shouted the goose.

The pig just grunted. Then the others hurriedly painted picket signs and marched around, shouting obscenities.

The government agent came and said to the little red hen, "You must not be greedy."

"But I earned the bread," said the little red hen.

"Exactly," said the agent. "That is the wonderful free enterprise system. Anyone in the barnyard can earn as much as he wants. But, under government regulations, the productive workers must divide their product with the idle."

They all lived happily ever after. But the little red hen's neighbors wondered why she never again baked bread.[2]

We leaders must be certain that our people don't feel like the little red hen. We must never be like the government agent. We must give positive acknowledgment and encouragement to the producers, and we must be careful not to reward the idle. Take a hard look at your organization. What are you rewarding?

ESTABLISH A SUPPORT SYSTEM

Develop a support system for employees. Nothing hurts morale more than asking people to do something and not giving them resources to accomplish it. I believe every potential leader needs support in five areas:

EMOTIONAL SUPPORT

Provide a "yes you can" atmosphere. Even when support is lacking in other areas, a person can forge ahead when given emotional support. This support costs the least and yields an incredible return.

SKILLS TRAINING

One of the fastest ways to build people up is to train them. People receiving training perceive that the organization believes in them. And they are more productive because they are more highly skilled.

MONEY

Stingy leaders produce stingy workers. It is difficult for people to give of themselves when their leader does not give of himself. If you pay peanuts, expect to get monkeys. Invest money in people; it always yields the highest return on your investment.

> **Invest money in people; it always yields the highest return on your investment.**

EQUIPMENT

To do the job right, you need the right tools. Too often a poor leader looks at things from a short-term perspective. Investing in the right equipment will give your people the time to be more productive, and it will keep up their morale.

PERSONNEL

Provide the people needed to get the job done. And provide good people. Personnel problems can eat up the time and energy of a potential leader, leaving little time for production.

Create a support system for all the people around you. But increase it for any individual only as he grows and is successful. I have found the familiar 80/20 principle that I discussed at length in *Developing the Leader Within You* holds especially true here. The top 20 percent of the people in the organization will perform 80 percent of the organization's production. So when structuring your support system, provide the top 20 percent producers with 80 percent of the total support.

People who have a support system have the environment and the tools to succeed. They are a part of a cooperative environment. A business training exercise, described in a speech by Tom Geddie of Central and Southwest Services, is a wonderful illustration of what can happen in a cooperative environment:

Draw an imaginary line on the floor, and put one person on each side. The purpose is to get one person to convince the other, without force, to cross the line. U.S. players almost never convince one another, but their Japanese counterparts simply say, "If you'll cross the line, so will I." They exchange places and they both win.

The Japanese recognize the important of cooperation and mutual support. It has been a key to their success in the last fifty years. It can be a key to your success and to that of the leaders around you.

DISCERN AND PERSONALIZE THE POTENTIAL LEADER'S JOURNEY

Teddy Roosevelt once had a little dog that was always getting in fights and always getting licked. Somebody said, "Colonel, he's not much of a fighter." Teddy replied, "Oh, he's a good fighter. He's just a poor judge of dogs."

Leaders must be good at judging others. Leadership expert Peter Drucker has often said, "It is important to disciple a life, not teach a lesson." Discipleship of another person involves discerning where that person is, knowing where he is supposed to go, and giving him what he needs to get there. The person and the assignments he is given must match. As Drucker says, people are much like flowers. One, like a rose, needs fertilizer. Another, more like a rhododendron, doesn't. If you don't give flowers the care they need, they'll never bloom. The leader must be able to tell which is which.

> **Spend 80 percent of your time on the most promising 20 percent of the potential leaders around you.**

In the previous chapter, we discussed the identification of potential leaders. Everyone you recruit for your organization should be a potential leader, but you should not try to personally mentor everyone in your organization. Lead and nurture everyone within your influence, but spend 80 percent of your time on the most promising 20 percent of the potential leaders around you. Here are some guidelines for selecting the right people to mentor and develop:

SELECT PEOPLE WHOSE PHILOSOPHY OF LIFE IS SIMILAR TO YOURS

It will be difficult to develop someone whose values are too different from yours.

CHOOSE PEOPLE WITH POTENTIAL YOU GENUINELY BELIEVE IN

If you don't believe in them, you won't give them the time they need. And they will discern your lack of confidence in them. Belief in their potential, on the other hand, will empower them. Some of the nation's greatest professional athletes have come from tiny colleges that receive no publicity. All those ball players needed was for pro scouts to recognize the potential that the right opportunity could bring out. The secret of mentoring in any field is to help a person get where he or she is willing to go.

DETERMINE WHAT THEY NEED

Determining what potential leaders need involves looking at their strengths and weaknesses objectively. Their strengths indicate the directions they need to go, what they can become. Their weaknesses show us what we need to help them improve. Encouraging them in their strengths and helping them overcome their weaknesses will move them closer to reaching their potential.

EVALUATE THEIR PROGRESS CONSTANTLY

People need feedback, especially early in their development. Ben Franklin said, "The eye of the master will do more work than both his hands." He knew that a leader's ability to evaluate is his greatest strength. An honest mentor will be objective. If necessary, he or she will encourage the person to stay on course, to seek another direction, or even to enter into a relationship with another mentor.

BE COMMITTED, SERIOUS, AND AVAILABLE TO THE PEOPLE YOU MENTOR

The development of the potential leaders will be a reflection of your commitment to them: poor commitment equals poor development; great commitment equals great development.

Danny Thomas said, "All of us are born for a reason, but all of us don't discover why. Success in life has nothing to do with what you gain in life or accomplish for yourself. It's what you do for others." By personalizing each person's journey, you are helping him to maximize his potential. You are giving him a chance to discover his purpose. You also maximize his contribution to you and your organization.

Most people agree that nurturing is important to the development of children. However, they often fail to see its importance in the workplace. They assume that potential leaders will nurture themselves. If we as leaders do not nurture the potential leaders around us, they will never develop into the types of leaders we desire. As Ralph Waldo Emerson said, "It is one of the most beautiful compensations of this life that no man can sincerely try to help another without helping himself." When you nurture the people around you, everyone wins.

FIVE

THE LEADER'S DAILY REQUIREMENT:
EQUIPPING POTENTIAL LEADERS

At this point you know how to identify potential leaders, how to create a climate in which they can be nurtured, and how to nurture them in some basic ways. It is time to look more specifically at how to prepare them for leadership within the organization. That preparation process is called equipping.

Equipping is similar to training. But I prefer the term "equipping" because it more accurately describes the process potential leaders must go through. Training is generally focused on specific job tasks; for instance, you train a person to use a copy machine or to answer a phone in a particular way. Training is only a part of the equipping process that prepares a person for leadership.

When I think of equipping a potential leader, I think of preparing an unskilled person to scale a tall mountain peak. His preparation is a process. Certainly he needs to be outfitted with equipment, such as cold-weather clothing, ropes, picks, and spikes. He also needs to be trained how to use that equipment.

A mountain climber's preparation, though, involves much more than simply having the correct equipment and knowing how to use it. The person must be conditioned physically to prepare him for the difficult climb. He must be trained to be a part of a team. Most important, he must be taught to *think* like a mountain climber. He needs to be able to look at a peak and *see* how it is to be conquered. Without going through the complete equipping process, he not only won't make it to the top of the mountain, but he also might find himself stranded on the side of the mountain, freezing to death.

> **Equipping, like nurturing, is an ongoing process.**

Equipping, like nurturing, is an ongoing process. You don't equip a person in a few hours or a day. And it can't be done using a formula or a videotape. Equipping must be tailored to each potential leader.

The ideal equipper is a person who can impart the vision of the work, evaluate the potential leader, give him the tools he needs, and then help him along the way at the beginning of his journey.

The equipper is a *model*—a leader who does the job, does it well, does it right, and does it with consistency.

The equipper is a *mentor*—an advisor who has the vision of the organization and can communicate it to others. He or she has experience to draw upon.

The equipper is an *empowerer*—one who can instill in the potential leader the desire and ability to do the work. He or she is able to lead, teach, and assess the progress of the person being equipped.

> **Equipping must be tailored to each potential leader.**

To see how your discernment skills measure up, take a look at this chart of potential leader characteristics adapted from author and leadership consultant Bobb Biehl:[1]

PERFORMANCE FACTORS	FAR EXCEEDS JOB REQUIREMENTS	EXCEEDS JOB REQUIREMENTS	MEETS JOB REQUIREMENTS	NEEDS SOME IMPROVEMENT	DOES NOT MEET MINIMUM REQUIREMENTS
Quality	Leaps tall buildings with a single bound	Must take running start to leap over tall buildings	Can only leap over a short building or medium with no spires	Crashes into buildings when attempting to jump over them	Cannot recognize building at all, much less jump
Timeliness	Is faster than a speeding bullet	Is as fast as a speeding bullet	Not quite as fast as a speeding bullet	Would you believe a slow bullet?	Wounds self with bullet when attempting to shoot gun
Initiative	Is stronger than a locomotive	Is stronger than an elephant	Is stronger than a bull	Shoots the bull	Smells like a bull
Adaptability	Walks on water consistently	Walks on water in emergencies	Washes with water	Drinks water	Passes water in emergencies
Communication	Talks with God	Talks with the angels	Talks to self	Argues with self	Loses those arguments

EQUIPPING QUESTIONS

Effective equipping begins with asking questions. We ask them to determine the direction our equipping efforts must take. If we don't, we may find ourselves teaching the wrong people the wrong things for the wrong purpose. I begin the process with analysis of the organization, myself, and the potential leaders. To get the information I need, I ask three sets of questions:

QUESTIONS ABOUT THE ORGANIZATION

These questions will determine what equipping needs to be done and the direction it should take to best serve the organization:

What is the statement of purpose for the organization? The development of leaders in an organization must begin with a review of the organization's purpose. (Presumably, the purpose of your organization is already in writing. If not, write it down. Or ask someone in authority to provide you with a statement of purpose.) Don't even consider performing equipping or training that does not contribute to the fulfillment of the organization's purpose.

What is the primary need of the organization? If you know what the organization needs most in order to fulfill its purpose, then you know its primary equipping need. Define that need as specifically as possible.

Is there a training program in place to meet that need? If there isn't, you know where to start. If there is, then use the ideas in this chapter to improve it.

What areas within the organization have the greatest growth potential? When you train and equip to prepare for growth, you play to your strengths. You are being proactive rather than reactive. You are putting yourself in a position to meet the future totally prepared.

Do those potential growth areas have the needed leaders to accomplish the task? Without leaders ready to make things happen, the area of growth potential will never move from "potential" to reality. If the leaders don't already exist, they will have to be equipped and developed.

QUESTIONS ABOUT MYSELF

The questions concerning the organization indicate the direction the equipping must take. This next set of questions will make clear how the equipping will be done. As the leader, I set the tone for the equipping process.

Am I willing to pour my life into others? Giving to potential leaders is a way of life for the best leaders. They do it daily. The development of their people is more important than the development of their own status. They are willing to share the credit when things go right. Equipping involves sacrifice.

Am I committed to an equipping organization? Equipping requires commitment. It takes time and effort on the part of an organization's leadership. Everyone knows it's quicker and easier for a leader to do a job himself than it is for him to teach other people to do it. But doing it yourself is a short-term solution. The longer, harder road of equipping others pays in the long run, but it requires commitment from everyone in the organization.

Am I effective in the areas I need to equip? This is a tough question that requires an honest answer. If the answer is "no," the leader must locate a person, inside or outside the organization, effective in those areas who can do some of the training. Either that, or he had better go out and get himself equipped.

Have I developed a prospect list of potential leaders? As I mentioned in Chapter Three, a good leader is always looking for potential leaders. You always begin with the best people you can. As you nurture them, a group of people with the most potential will emerge. From that group, draw up a prospect list of potential leaders to be considered for equipping and development.

What assumptions have I made that need to be changed? People often get a false first impression of other people. Many times leaders build their expectations of the people they will develop on assumptions from those false first impressions. When you are aware that you have made some assumptions, you can go beyond the superficial and move to a new level in your relationships with your potential leaders. It allows you to better understand where they are, what they need, and what you can provide them.

QUESTIONS ABOUT THE POTENTIAL LEADER

Once you have identified the organization's equipping needs, examined yourself, and developed a prospect list, you are ready to select the people to be equipped. The goal now is to narrow the field of prospective leaders down to the few people with the most potential. Ask yourself these questions about each person to find the ones with the highest potential:

Is this person compatible philosophically with the organization and my leadership? If the answer is no, don't even consider equipping or mentoring this person. There must be compatibility first; otherwise, no amount of training in the world will make this person the type of leader you want and need.

Does this person show a potential for growth? Potential for growth does not guarantee growth, but a lack of growth potential guarantees no growth will occur. If the person does not appear to have the desire and the ability to grow, look for another candidate.

Are there lingering questions I have about this person? The time to have lingering questions answered is before the person is selected for equipping. Take time to interview, then do follow-up interviews to answer other questions that occur to you later. You may want to have someone you respect in your organization do an interview as well. He or she will sometimes see things you missed. If you can positively answer 95 percent of your questions about this person, then the person is probably a good candidate. The one exception is character. If you have any lingering questions concerning his character, don't choose him for development.

Am I selecting this person because of obvious strengths or because I don't see any glaring weaknesses? When you look at a potential leader and don't see even one great strength, don't choose him for equipping and development—even if you see no great weaknesses. As tempting as it may be to select that person, don't do it. Why? Because if you do, you are asking for mediocrity.

Management expert Peter Drucker, in *The Effective Executive*, explains that Abraham Lincoln made this mistake early in his presidency when selecting generals. He sought men without glaring weaknesses. As a result, the well-equipped Union army fared poorly against the Confederates. Lincoln once remarked irritably that if General McClellen didn't plan to use the army, he would like to borrow it for a while.

The Confederate army was staffed with generals who, although they had obvious weaknesses, were picked for their great and obvious strengths. These strengths, properly developed and applied, gave them victory after victory. Lincoln finally learned this lesson and selected as leader of the Union army Ulysses Grant, a great general, but also an alcoholic. When you look for potential leaders, select people with obvious strengths even if you see weaknesses.

What is the potential leader's fit? There are two kinds of "fit" to consider. First, a person's gifts and abilities must fit the job he is to perform. Consider such gifts and abilities as temperament, background, job experiences, skills, personality, and passion. People need to be trained and developed primarily in their areas of strength. And most of the work they are asked to do should be in those areas. I often talk about the 80/20 principle, and it applies here as well. A person should be spending 80 percent of his time doing things that require his greatest gifts and abilities. This will help keep him fulfilled.

The second has to do with how well he will fit into the team. No matter how great the player, if he can't play with the team, he won't help the organization. The addition of a new team member always changes the chemistry of the team.

> **A person should be spending 80 percent of his time doing things that require his greatest gifts and abilities.**

It's obvious in sports: A good team is made up of people with different talents playing different positions to accomplish one goal. (Can you imagine a whole basketball team of seven-foot centers who specialize in blocking shots—no shooting guards, no shooting or rebounding forwards, and no playmakers—just centers? What a disaster.)

Teams outside of sports need to be created strategically too. They must have the right chemistry. When each player brings his particular style and talents to the team, and they come together with respect and appreciation for one another, it can create a wonderful and powerful team.

If you haven't already stopped to answer these questions, I want to encourage you to do so right now. Write down your answers. If you have your own organization, you cannot afford to let any more time go by without preparing for your organization's future. Even if you are not the CEO of the organization, you can still apply these principles. Do it now!

HOW TO EQUIP FOR EXCELLENCE

Now that you know who you are going to equip and for what you are going to equip them, you are ready to get started. The steps that follow will take you through the whole process. They begin with building relationships with your potential leaders. From that foundation, you can build programs for their development, supervise their progress, empower them to do the jobs, and finally get them to pass on the legacy.

DEVELOP A PERSONAL RELATIONSHIP WITH THE PEOPLE YOU EQUIP

All good mentoring relationships begin with a personal relationship. As your people get to know and like you, their desire to follow your direction and learn from you will increase. If they don't like you, they will not want to learn from you, and the equipping process slows down or even stops.

To build relationships, begin by listening to people's life stories, their journeys so far. Your genuine interest in them will mean a lot to them. It will also help you to know their personal strengths and weaknesses. Ask them about their goals and what motivates them. Find out what kind of temperaments they

> **All good mentoring relationships begin with a personal relationship.**

have. You certainly don't want to equip and develop a person whose greatest love is numbers and financial statements for a position where he would be spending 80 percent of his time dealing with disgruntled customers.

One of the best ways to get to know people is to see them outside of the business world. People are usually on their guard at work. They try to be what others want them to be. By getting to know them in other settings, you can get to know who they really are. Try to learn as much as you can about the people and do your best to win their hearts. If you first find their hearts, they'll be glad to give you their hands.

SHARE YOUR DREAM

While getting to know your people, share your dream. It helps them to know you and where you're going. There's no act that will better show them your heart and your motivation.

Woodrow Wilson once said,

We grow by dreams. All big individuals are dreamers. They see things in the soft haze of a spring day, or in the red fire on a long winter's evening. Some of us let those great dreams die, but others nourish and protect them; nourish them through bad days until they bring them to the sunshine and light which comes always to those who sincerely hope that their dreams will come true.

I have often wondered, "Does the person make the dream or does the dream make the person?" My conclusion is both are equally true.

All good leaders have a dream. All great leaders share their dream with others who can help them make it a reality. As Florence Littauer suggests, we must:

Dare to dream:	Have the desire to do something bigger than yourself.
Prepare the dream:	Do your homework; be ready when the opportunity comes.
Wear the dream:	Do it.
Share the dream:	Make others a part of the dream, and it will become even greater than you had hoped.

ASK FOR COMMITMENT

In his book *The One Minute Manager*, Ken Blanchard says, "There's a difference between interest and commitment. When you are interested in doing something, you do it only when it is convenient. When you are committed to something, you accept no excuses." Don't equip people who are merely interested. Equip the ones who are committed.

Commitment is the one quality above all others that enables a potential leader to become a successful leader. Without commitment, there can be no success. Football coach Lou Holtz recognized the difference between being merely involved and being truly committed. He pointed out, "The kamikaze pilot that was able to fly 50 missions was involved—but never committed."

To determine whether your people are committed, first you must make sure they know what it will cost them to become leaders. That means that you must be sure not to undersell the job—let them know what it's going to take. Only then will they know what they are committing to. If they won't commit, don't go any further in the equipping process. Don't waste your time.

SET GOALS FOR GROWTH

People need clear objectives set before them if they are to achieve anything of value. Success never comes instantaneously. It comes from taking many small steps. A set of goals becomes a map a potential leader can follow in order to grow. As Shad Helmsetter states in *You Can Excel in Time of Change*, "It is the goal that shapes the plan; it is the plan that sets the action; it is the action that achieves the result; and it is the result that brings the success. And it all begins with the simple word *goal*." We, as equipping leaders, must introduce our people to the practice of setting and achieving goals.

Lily Tomlin once said, "I always wanted to be somebody, but I should have been more specific." Many people today find themselves in the same situation. They have some vague idea of what success is, and they know they want to achieve it. But they haven't worked out any kind of plan to get there. I have found that the greatest achievers in life are people who set goals for themselves and then work hard to reach them. What they *get* by reaching the goals is not nearly as important as what they *become* by reaching them.

When you help your people set goals, use the following guidelines:

Make the goals appropriate. Always keep in mind the job you want the people to do and the desired result: the development of your people into effective leaders. Identify goals that will contribute to that larger goal.

Make the goals attainable. Nothing will make people want to quit faster than facing unachievable goals. I like the comment made by Ian MacGregor, former AMAX Corporation chairman of the board: "I work on the same principle as people who train horses. You start with low fences, easily achieved goals, and work up. It's important in management never to ask people to try to accomplish goals they can't accept."

Make the goals measurable. Your potential leaders will never know when they have achieved their goals if they aren't measurable. When they are measurable, the knowledge that they have been attained will give them a sense of accomplishment. It will also free them to set new goals in place of the old ones.

Clearly state the goals. When goals have no clear focus, neither will the actions of the people trying to achieve them.

Make the goals require a "stretch." As I mentioned before, goals have to be achievable. On the other hand, when goals don't require a stretch, the people achieving them won't grow. The leader must know his people well enough to identify attainable goals that require a stretch.

> The leader must know his people well enough to identify attainable goals that require a stretch.

Put the goals in writing. When people write down their goals, it makes them more accountable for those goals. A study of a Yale University graduating class showed that the small percentage of graduates who had written down their goals accomplished more than all of the other graduates combined. Putting goals in writing works.

It is also important to encourage your potential leaders to review their goals and progress frequently. Ben Franklin set aside time every day to review two questions. In the morning he asked himself, "What good shall I do today?" In the evening he asked, "What good have I done today?"

COMMUNICATE THE FUNDAMENTALS

For people to be productive and satisfied professionally, they have to know what their fundamental responsibilities are. It sounds so simple, but Peter Drucker says one of the critical problems in the workplace today is that there is a lack of understanding between the employer and employee as to what the employee is to do. Often employees are made to feel they are vaguely responsible for everything. It paralyzes them. Instead, we need to make clear to them what they *are* and *are not* responsible for. Then they will be able to focus their efforts on what we want, and they will succeed.

Look again at how a basketball team works. Each of the five players has a particular job. There is a shooting guard whose job is to score points. The other guard is a point guard. His job is to pass the ball to people who can score. Another player is a power forward who is expected to get rebounds. The small forward's job is to score. The center is supposed to rebound, block shots, and score. Each person on the team knows what his job is, what his unique contribution to the team must be. When each concentrates on his particular responsibilities, the team can win.

One of the best ways to clarify expectations is to provide your people with job descriptions. In the description, identify the four to six primary functions you want the person to perform. Avoid long laundry lists of responsibilities. If the job description can't be summarized, the job is probably too broad. Also try to make clear what authority they have, the working parameters for each function they are to perform, and what the chain of authority is within the organization.

Another essential that has to be communicated to new leaders is how they are to prioritize. I tell people that everything they do is either an "A" or a "B" priority. The concept helps them understand what is most important.

"A" priorities are ones that move the organization, department, or job function forward. They break ground, open doors to new opportunities, or develop new markets. They promote growth within people or the organization. "B" priorities are concerned with maintenance. They are required for things to continue running smoothly, such as answering letters or phone calls, and taking care of details. They are things that cannot be neglected, but they don't add value to the organization. I have found that people often expend their best on "B" priorities because they seem urgent, and they give "A" priorities what's left over. I always encourage my people to give 80 percent of their time and energy to the "A" priorities and the remaining 20 percent to the "B" group.

Finally, a leader must communicate to his or her people that their work has value to the organization and to the individual leader. To the employee, this often is the most important fundamental of all.

PERFORM THE FIVE-STEP PROCESS OF TRAINING PEOPLE

Part of the equipping process includes training people to perform the specific tasks of the jobs they are to do. The approach the leader takes to training will largely determine his people's success or failure. If he takes a dry, academic approach, the potential leaders will remember little of what's taught. If he simply throws the people into the job without any direction, they may feel like this employee of Hagar the Horrible:

Reprinted with special permission of King Features Syndicate

The best type of training takes advantage of the way people learn. Researchers tell us that we remember 10 percent of what we hear,

50 percent of what we see, 70 percent of what we say, and 90 percent of what we hear, see, say, and do. Knowing that, we have to develop an approach to how we will train. I have found the best training method to be a five-step process:

Step 1: I model. The process begins with my doing the tasks while the person being trained watches. When I do this, I try to give the person an opportunity to see me go through the whole process. Too often when leaders train, they begin in the middle of the task and confuse the people they're trying to teach. When people see the task performed correctly and completely, it gives them something to try to duplicate.

Step 2: I mentor. During this next step, I continue to perform the task, but this time the person I'm training comes alongside me and assists in the process. I also take time to explain not only the *how* but also the *why* of each step.

Step 3: I monitor. We exchange places this time. The trainee performs the task and I assist and correct. It's especially important during this phase to be positive and encouraging to the trainee. It keeps him trying and it makes him want to improve rather than give up. Work with him until he develops consistency. Once he's gotten down the process, ask him to explain it to you. It will help him to understand and remember.

Step 4: I motivate. I take myself out of the task at this point and let the trainee go. My task is to make sure he knows how to do it without help and to keep encouraging him so he will continue to improve. It is important for me to stay with him until he senses success. It's a great motivator. At this time the trainee may want to make improvements to the process. Encourage him to do it, and at the same time learn from him.

Step 5: I multiply. This is my favorite part of the whole process. Once the new leaders do the job well, it becomes their turn to teach others how to do it. As teachers know, the best way to learn something is to teach it. And the beauty of this is it frees me to do other important developmental tasks while others carry on the training.

GIVE THE "BIG THREE"

All the training in the world will provide limited success if you don't turn your people loose to do the job. I believe that if I get the best people, give them my vision, train them in the basics, and then let go, I will get a high return from them. As General George S. Patton once remarked, "Never tell people how to do things. Tell them what to do and they will surprise you with their ingenuity."

You can't turn people loose without structure, but you also want to give them enough freedom to be creative. The way to do that is to give them the big three: *responsibility, authority,* and *accountability*.

For some people, responsibility is the easiest of the three to give. We all want the people around us to be responsible. We know how important it is. As author/editor Michael Korda said, "Success on any major scale requires you to accept responsibility. . . . In the final analysis, the one quality that all successful people have . . . is the ability to take on responsibility."

What is more difficult for some leaders is allowing their people to keep the responsibility after it's been given. Poor managers want to control every detail of their people's work. When that happens, the potential leaders who work for them become frustrated and don't develop. Rather than desiring more responsibility, they become indifferent or avoid responsibility altogether. If you want your people to take responsibility, truly give it to them.

With responsibility must go authority. Progress does not come unless they are given together. Winston Churchill, while addressing the House of Commons during the Second World War, said, "I am your servant. You have the right to dismiss me when you please. What you have no right to do is ask me to bear responsibility without the power of action." When responsibility and authority come together, people become genuinely empowered.

There's an important aspect of authority that needs to be noted. When we first give authority to new leaders, we are actually *giving them permission* to have authority rather than *giving them authority* itself. True authority has to be earned. George Davis, in *Magic Shortcuts to Executive Success*, notes:

> Authority is not something we buy, are born with, or even have delegated to us by our superiors. It is something we earn—and we earn it from our subordinates. No manager has any real authority over his people until he has proved himself worthy of it—in the eyes of his people—not his own, nor those of his superiors.

We must give our people permission to develop authority. That is our responsibility. They, in turn, must take responsibility for earning it.

I have found there are different levels of authority:

Position. The most basic kind of authority comes from a person's position on the organizational chart. This type of authority does not extend beyond the parameters of the job description. This is where all new leaders start. From here they may either earn greater authority, or they can minimize what little authority they have been given. It's up to them.

Competence. This type of authority is based on a person's professional capabilities, the ability to do a job. Followers give competent leaders authority within the leader's area of expertise.

Personality. Followers will also give authority to people based on their personal characteristics, such as personality, appearance, and charisma. Authority based on personality is a little broader than competence-based authority, but it is not really more advanced because it tends to be superficial.

Integrity. Authority based on integrity comes from a person's core. It is based on character. When new leaders gain authority based on their integrity, they have crossed into a new stage of their development.

Spirituality. In secular circles, people rarely consider the power of spiritual-based authority. It comes from people's individual experiences with God and from His power working through them. It is the highest form of authority.

Leaders must earn authority with each new group of people. However, I have found that once leaders have gained authority on a particular level, it takes very little time for them to establish that level of authority with another group of people. The higher the level of authority, the more quickly it happens.

Once responsibility and authority have been given to people, they are empowered to make things happen. But we also have to be sure they are making the right things happen. That's where accountability comes into the picture. True responsibility on the part of new leaders includes a willingness to be held accountable. If we are providing them the right climate (as described in Chapter Two), our people will not fear accountability. They will admit mistakes and see them as a part of the learning process.

The leader's part of accountability involves taking the time to review the new leader's work and give honest, constructive criticism. It is crucial that the leader be supportive but honest. It's been said that when Harry Truman was thrust into the presidency upon the death of President Franklin D. Roosevelt, Speaker of the House Sam Rayburn gave him some fatherly advice: "From here on out you're going to have lots of people around you. They'll try to put a wall around you and cut you off from any ideas but theirs. They'll tell you what a great man you are, Harry. But you and I both know you ain't." Rayburn was holding President Truman accountable.

GIVE THEM THE TOOLS THEY NEED

Giving responsibility without resources is ridiculous; it is incredibly limiting. Abraham Maslow said, "If the only tool you have is a hammer, you tend to see every problem as a nail." If we want our people to be creative and resourceful, we need to provide resources.

Obviously, the most basic tools are pieces of equipment, such as copying machines, computers, and whatever else simplifies someone's work. We must be sure not only to provide everything necessary for a job to be done, but also equipment that will allow jobs, especially "B" priorities, to be done more quickly and efficiently. Always work toward freeing people's time for important things.

Tools, however, include much more than equipment. It is important to provide developmental tools. Spend time mentoring people in specific areas of need. Be willing to spend money on things like books, tapes, seminars, and professional conferences. There is a wealth of good information out there, and fresh ideas from outside an organization can stimulate growth. Be creative in providing tools. It will keep your people growing and equip them to do the job well.

CHECK ON THEM SYSTEMATICALLY

I believe in touching base with people frequently. I like to give mini-evaluations all the time. Leaders who wait to give feedback only during annual formal evaluations are asking for trouble. People need the encouragement of being told they're doing well on a regular basis. They also need to hear as soon as possible when they are not doing well. It prevents a lot of problems with the organization, and it improves the leader.

How often I check on people is determined by a number of factors:

The importance of the task. When something is critical to the success of the organization, I touch base often.

The demands of the work. I find that if the work is very demanding, the person performing it needs encouragement more often. He may also need questions answered or need help solving difficult problems. Occasionally, when the job is really tough, I tell the person to take a break—demanding work can lead a person to burnout.

The newness of the work. Some leaders have no problem tackling a new task, no matter how different it is from previous work. Others have great difficulty adapting. I check often on the people who are less flexible or creative.

The newness of the worker. I want to give new leaders every possible chance to succeed. So I check on newer people more often. That way I can help them anticipate problems and make sure that they have a series of successes. By that they gain confidence.

The responsibility of the worker. When I know I can give a person a task and it will always get done, I may not check on that person until the task is complete. With less responsible people, I can't afford to do that.

My approach to checking on people also varies from person to person. For instance, rookies and veterans should be treated differently. But no matter how long people have been with me, there are some things I always do:

Discuss feelings. I always give my people an opportunity to tell me how they feel. I also tell them how I'm feeling. It clears the air and makes it possible for us to get down to business.

Measure progress. Together, we try to determine their progress. I often ask questions to find out what I need to know. If people are hitting obstacles, I remove the ones I can.

Give feedback. This is a critical part of the process. I always give them some kind of evaluation. I'm honest, and I do my homework to make sure I'm accurate. I give constructive criticism. This lets them know how they're doing, corrects problems, encourages improvements, and speeds the work.

Give encouragement. Whether the person is doing well or poorly, I always give encouragement. I encourage poor performers to do better. I encourage peak performers. I praise milestones. I try to give hope and encouragement when people are experiencing personal issues. Encouragement keeps people going.

Though it doesn't happen very often, I occasionally have a person whose progress is repeatedly poor. When that happens, I try to determine what's gone wrong. Usually poor performance is a result of one of three things: (1) a mismatch between the job and the person; (2) inadequate training or leadership; or (3) deficiencies in the person performing the work. Before I take any action, I always try to determine what the issues are. I line up my facts to be sure there really is a deficiency in performance and not just a problem with my perception. Next I define as precisely as possible what the deficiency is. Finally, I check with the person who is not performing to get the other side of the story.

Once I've done my homework, I try to determine where the deficiency is. If it's a mismatch, I explain the problem to the person, move him to a place that fits, and reassure him of my confidence in him. If the problem involves training or leadership issues, I back up and redo whatever step hasn't been performed properly. Once again, I let the person know what the problem was and give him plenty of encouragement. If the problem is with the person, I sit down with him and let him know about it. I make it clear where his failures are and what he must do to overcome them. Then I give him another chance. But I also begin the documentation process in case I have to fire him. I want him to succeed, but I will waste no time letting him go if he doesn't do what it takes to improve.

CONDUCT PERIODIC EQUIPPING MEETINGS

Even after you've completed most of your people's training and are preparing to take them into their next growth phase—development—continue to conduct periodic equipping meetings. It helps your people stay on track, helps them keep growing, and encourages them to begin taking responsibility for equipping themselves.

When I prepare an equipping meeting, I include the following:

Good news. I always start on a positive note. I review the good things that are happening in the organization and pay particular attention to their areas of interest and responsibility.

Vision. People can get so caught up in their day-to-day responsibilities that they lose sight of the vision that drives the organization. Use the opportunity of an equipping meeting to recast that vision. It will also give them the appropriate context for the training you are about to give.

Content. Content will depend on their needs. Try to focus training on areas that will help them in the "A" priority areas, and orient the training on the people, not the lesson.

Administration. Cover any organizational items that give the people a sense of security and encourage their leadership.

Empowerment. Take time to connect with the people you equip. Encourage them personally. And show them how the equipping session empowers them to perform their jobs better. They will leave the meeting feeling positive and ready to work.

The entire equipping process takes a lot of time and attention. It requires more time and dedication from the equipping leader than mere training. But its focus is long term, not short term. Rather than creating followers or even adding new leaders, it multiplies leaders. As I explained in the section on the five-step process of equipping, it is not complete until the equipper and the new leader select someone for the new leader to train. It is only then that the equipping process has come full circle. Without a successor, there can be no success.

Leaders who are equipping others have the greatest possibility of success, no matter what type of organization they're in. When a leader is dedicated to the equipping process, the whole level of performance within the organization rises dramatically. Everyone is better prepared to get the work done. More important, the best-equipped people will be ready for the final growth stage that creates the very best leaders—development. As Fred A. Manske, Jr. said, "The greatest leader is willing to train people and develop them to the point that they eventually surpass him or her in knowledge and ability." The following chapter will show you how to take that step.

SIX

THE LEADER'S LIFELONG COMMITMENT:
DEVELOPING POTENTIAL LEADERS

If you have done all the things I've discussed so far in this book—created a great environment, nurtured your people, and equipped the best people around you—your achievements have already surpassed those of the majority of managers in the work force today. You can consider yourself a better-than-average leader. If you go no further, though, you will never become a *great* leader. No matter how hard or how smart you work, you will never become one of the best of the best. Why? Because the very best leaders, the top 1 percent, take their people the next step and develop them so they can reach their potential. The growth and development of people is the highest calling of leadership.

You're probably wondering why most leaders don't take this final step. They don't because it's hard work. I once heard the story of a preacher who quit the ministry after twenty years and became a funeral director. When asked why he made the change, he replied, "Well, I spent three years trying to straighten out Fred, and Fred is still an alcoholic. And I spent six

> **The growth and development of people is the highest calling of leadership.**

months trying to straighten out Susan's marriage, and she filed for divorce. Then I spent over two-and-a-half years trying to straighten out Bob's drug problem, and he's still an addict. Now at the funeral home, when I straighten them out—they stay straight."

Living, breathing human beings require continual attention. And development is demanding work. It takes more attention and commitment than either nurturing or equipping. To see the differences in emphasis in nurturing, equipping, and developing, look at the following table:

NURTURING	EQUIPPING	DEVELOPING
Care	Training for Work	Training for Personal Growth
Focus Is on Need	Focus Is on Task	Focus Is on Person
Relational	Transactional	Transformational
Service	Management	Leadership
Maintains Leadership	Adds Leadership	Multiplies Leadership
Establishing	Releasing	Empowering
Helping	Teaching	Mentoring
Need Oriented	Skill Oriented	Character Oriented
What They Want	What the Organization Needs	What They Need
A Desire	A Science	An Art
Little or No Growth	Short-Term Growth	Long-Term Growth
All	Many	Few

Take a look at the qualities associated with developing leaders. They are based on what the potential leaders need, on their growth. The process is designed to build into them, to bring out their best qualities, to develop their character, and to help them discover and reach their potential.

Because the development of leaders requires time, attention, and commitment, a developer can only work with a few people at a time, as the last entry in the table indicates. Nurture all of your people, and equip many. But develop only a few—the few who are ready and willing.

There is another important difference between equipping and developing people. Equipping is essentially a step-by-step process. You can take people through specific steps to equip them. That is the *science* of equipping. Leadership development is more of an *art*. It is not a series of specific steps that you take people through. Instead, there are aspects that must be addressed throughout the whole process.

Here are the twelve actions a leader must take to develop potential leaders into the best they can be.

ASK THE THREE MOTIVATION QUESTIONS

All growth begins with motivation. You as the developer must find your potential leaders' motivations and harness them. Begin by asking these questions:

WHAT DO THEY WANT?

Everyone wants something. Even the person who appears not to be motivated has desires. You need to find out what your people want. Sometimes they will tell you. Other times you need to use discernment. Since you will have already built relationships with them, use information that you've learned during your personal interactions with them. No matter how, you need to find out what will motivate them to develop.

Do They Have a Way of Getting What They Want?

Whenever people want something but see no way to get it, they will not be motivated. One of your jobs as the leader is to determine how your potential leaders can achieve what they desire and show them a way to do it. Because you have already traveled the road of achievement, you may be able to see the way more clearly and can help point the way. Sometimes you may even have the power to create a way for them to achieve what they want on a personal level.

Will They Be Rewarded if Successful?

Sometimes even people who have goals and see ways of achieving them lack motivation. Why? Because they don't believe the rewards will outweigh the work required to achieve them. As their leader, you can share from your own experience that the rewards are worth the effort. You are also in a position to show them how their personal goals and desires coincide with those of the organization. When both have the same goals, the rewards are multiplied.

For example, if the goal of one of your people is to become an outstanding salesperson, that goal also benefits the organization, and the organization will reward it (in commission or salary). As a result, if that person achieves that goal, he will receive the personal benefits to himself as well as the monetary rewards from the organization. The rewards are multiplied.

> **Good leaders are good listeners.**

Ask the questions to find your people's motivation, and then harness that motivation to help them develop.

BE A GOOD LISTENER

Good leaders are good listeners. Listening to your people will add to your success and to their development. When you listen to their ideas and opinions, especially before you make decisions, you give them a chance to increase their contribution. Each time you use their ideas and give them credit, they will feel valued, and they will be encouraged to keep contributing. This is one of the best ways to get them to start thinking creatively. They will also develop judgment and begin to understand the reasons why you use some of their ideas and choose not to use others. They will learn to see things more clearly and more in terms of the big picture.

The critical aspect of this process is that you genuinely seek their advice and then listen to their views actively and positively. If you are simply going through the motions, your people will know it. Likewise, never criticize the person making a suggestion, even if it's a poor one. People who feel belittled will soon stop

> **Every idea is a good idea until you've settled on the best idea.**

making suggestions, and you may miss out on their next great idea because you've discouraged them from contributing. Try to adopt this attitude: every idea is a good idea until you've settled on the best idea.

DEVELOP A PLAN FOR PERSONAL GROWTH

One of the things I enjoy most is doing conferences around the country. I especially love the five or six leadership conferences sponsored each year through our organization INJOY. One of the most important things I talk about at those conferences is personal growth.

I often invite anyone in the audience who has already created a personal plan for growth to come up during the break to tell me about it. Do you know that in all the years I have been doing that, not once has anyone come up to me. Why? Because not one had created a personal growth plan for himself.

People think personal growth is a natural result of being alive. Well it's not. Growth is not automatic; it does not necessarily come with experience, nor simply as a result of gathering information. Personal growth must be deliberate, planned, and consistent.

One of the best things you can do for the people you are developing, besides modeling personal growth yourself, is to help them develop their own personal plans for growth. I want to emphasize that growth requires a *plan*. As my friend Zig Ziglar says, "You were born to be a winner, but to be a winner you must plan to win and prepare to win." Growing is the same. You have to create a plan and follow it.

I have devoted the greater part of my life to my own personal development and the creation of materials for the personal development of others. I have created leadership development lessons every month since 1985, and sent them out to people across the country through INJOY and Maximum Impact, because my greatest desire is to help others reach their potential. That is why I hold leadership conferences. Let me outline for you a plan for growth that I give people at these conferences. Help your people adapt it to their needs. And use it yourself if you aren't already using another plan that works for you.

PRACTICAL STEPS FOR PERSONAL GROWTH

SET ASIDE TIME DAILY FOR GROWTH

There are two important concepts in this step. First, time for growth must be *planned*. Getting sidetracked is one of the easiest things in the world to do. Growth time that is not strategically planned into the day soon disappears because our lives are busy. People must find a time that works for them and schedule it into their calendar. Then they must guard that time as they would any other appointment. Second, the time set aside must be set aside daily—for no fewer than five days a week. Educators report that people learn more effectively in shorter regular sessions than long, infrequent blocks of time. A daily discipline pays dividends. Here is the weekly plan that I recommend at my conferences:

Monday:	One hour with God
Tuesday:	One hour listening to a leadership tape
Wednesday:	Another hour with the same tape (including time filing notes on highlights and reflecting on what has been learned)
Thursday:	One hour reading a leadership book
Friday:	Another hour with the same book (including time filing notes on highlights and reflecting on what has been learned)

Besides the daily plan, I also recommend going through materials during times that other people normally consider wasted time. For instance, whenever I travel, I take along books and magazines that may not be as meaty as my daily reading but that have good material. If I'm waiting in an airport or flying on a plane, I'm also reviewing material and clipping out useful articles and quotes.

FILE QUICKLY WHAT YOU LEARN

Every good piece of information a person finds needs to be processed and filed. I have used this system for more than thirty-five years. As I find good articles or quotes, I clip and file them. This has two advantages. First, whenever I need materials for a talk or seminar, I have thirty-five years of collected resources to draw upon. Second, each time I reduce an article down to its one most relevant sentence or paragraph, I have processed through all the information, digested it, summarized it, and learned it.

APPLY QUICKLY WHAT YOU LEARN

Simply knowing a thing will not make it a part of you. To do that, you must apply it. Each time you learn something new, it's good to ask yourself, "Where, when, and how can I use this?" I prefer to do more than simply make a mental connection with the things I learn, so I use this system:

- Select one thing each week that I've learned.

- Put it on a 3 x 5 card. (I keep it in front of me for a week.)

- Share it with my wife.

- Share it with someone else within twenty-four hours.

- Teach it to someone else. (I put it in a lesson.)

GROW WITH SOMEONE

I have a number of people around me who share things with me and whom I deliberately share things with. When you share what you are learning with others, it increases your insight, builds your relationship with them, gives you a common vision, and holds you accountable. It also creates worthwhile conversation.

PLAN YOUR GROWTH AND FOLLOW IT FOR A YEAR

The five-day plan outlined previously was designed to be followed throughout the year. Using that plan, you can easily read twelve books and listen to fifty-two tapes per year. At the end of a year, you will have tremendous resources to draw on and will have grown tremendously. If you want to become an expert in a subject, according to Earl Nightengale, spend an hour a day for five years focusing on that subject.

There's one more thing I must say about developing a plan for your people's growth: Start them today! People may tell you that they are too old to start now, that they're too busy to start now, or that the timing isn't right. Personal growth is like investing. It's not your *timing*. It's your *time in*. Get them going now.

> **Personal growth is like investing. It's not your *timing*. It's your *time in*.**

KEEP THE GROWTH GOING

We live in a competitive society that focuses on making it. Baseball players live for the day they make it to the big leagues. Business people climb the corporate ladder with the hope of someday being the CEO or chairman of the board. A few of the businesses that use network-marketing techniques propose the idea that if a person builds a big enough organization, he or she can sit back and let others do the work. The individual will have made it; he will have arrived. But the idea of arriving is an illusion. Our society is filled with people who arrive somewhere only to find themselves as discontented as they were before they succeeded. The point of the journey is not arriving. The point is what you learn and whom you become along the way. Having goals is positive. Thinking that our journey is over once we achieve some of them is a danger we all face.

John Wooden, one of the most successful basketball coaches of all time, focused on the growing process. In *Six Timeless Marketing*

Blunders, William L. Shanklin writes about Wooden's approach to coaching. Shanklin tells that while Wooden coached UCLA, he did not stress winning. He emphasized preparation, teamwork, a willingness to change, and the desire for each person to perform at peak potential. His focus was on the process, not the end product.

The same thing is true in industry. From a quality-control expert I heard, "In quality control, we are not concerned about the product. We are concerned about the process. If the process is right, the product is guaranteed." The same is true when it comes to personal growth.

As the developers of leaders, we must keep our people growing. We must model growth, encourage it, and reward it. We must show our people how to keep growing for the long haul. They are to be like trees which grow their entire lives. There is no such thing as a full-grown tree. The day a tree stops growing is the day it dies.

USE THE FOUR-STAGE PROCESS OF ADAPTATION

It takes most people time to adopt new ideas and adapt to new situations. They usually have to go through four stages before new concepts become their own. I have found that they usually accept things in this order:

VISUALLY

Most people are visual. They usually have to see something new in order to understand it.

EMOTIONALLY

After people see something new, then they respond to it emotionally. Give them time to work through their emotions before going on to the next phase.

EXPERIENTIALLY

Once people understand something and have accepted it emotionally, they are ready to give it a try. Experience enables them to reach the final phase.

CONVICTIONALLY

After people see something, accept it emotionally, and experience it positively, it becomes truly a part of their thinking, their belief systems.

If you are aware of these phases, you will be able to bring people along in their development without as many obstacles.

FOLLOW THE IDEA GRID

Even though you will be helping your people create a personal growth plan and encouraging them to do as much growing as possible on their own, you will also need to teach them yourself. Ideally, you will share with them what you are learning in your own development. I continue to do this with the people in my organization. The best method I have found is represented in the following acronym:

I *nstruction*

D *emonstration*

E *xposure*

A *ccountability*

First I instruct my people in a life-related context. Any idea or theory that cannot be applied to real life is useless. Besides, if it can't be applied to real life, I wouldn't be able to demonstrate it, which is my next step. By actually living and demonstrating any idea before

I present it to others, I am able to test it, better able to learn it, and better qualified to teach it. Next I expose my people to actual experience. Once they have heard and seen it, they are ready to try it themselves. Finally, I make sure there is accountability for them, either with me or with each other. If you don't set some kind of accountability, your people may think the ideas are great, but they may forget to use them. And when people are held accountable for using them, the ideas become a part of them.

— GIVE THEM VARIED EXPERIENCES

People resist change. If given a chance to do something comfortable and easy that they've done before versus the chance to do something difficult and new, most people will take the safe, easy route. As leaders, we can't let our people become complacent.

Varied experiences add incredibly to people's development. It keeps them growing, stretching, and learning. The broader people's base of experience, the better they will be at handling new challenges, solving problems, and overcoming difficult situations. In my organization, we have a three-year rule. Our leaders must change a significant number of their major duties and responsibilities every three years. It forces them to gain new skills. It gives newer leaders the opportunity to develop by having them step into new areas of responsibility. It allows older leaders to tackle new challenges. And it enhances everyone's creativity.

It is often tempting for us to leave successful people where they are—to keep them in the same jobs. But we must keep in mind that we are doing more than just getting the job done well. We are building leaders, and that takes extra effort and time. Angus J. MacQueen tells a story about James Garfield that illustrates this point. He says that prior to becoming President of the Unites States, Garfield was principal of Hiram College in Ohio. When a father asked if the course of study couldn't be simplified so his son might finish school sooner, Garfield replied, "Certainly. But it all depends upon what you want to make of your boy. When God wants to make an oak tree, He takes a hundred years. When He wants to make a squash, He requires only two months." Give your leaders deep, broad roots by growing them slowly and varying their experiences.

STRIVE FOR EXCELLENCE

Vince Lombardi, a great leader and one of the best ever to coach professional football, once said, "The quality of a person's life is in direct proportion to their commitment to excellence, regardless of their chosen field of endeavor." Lombardi recognized the importance of striving for excellence. And he was able to instill that desire in the people he coached.

When you strive for excellence, you prompt your people to shoot for the top. When a leader's goal is acceptability rather than excellence, then even the best people in the organization will produce what is merely acceptable. The rest may not even produce the minimum. When excellence is the standard, the best will hit the mark, and the others will at least hit the board.

Another advantage of focusing on excellence is that it shows your people's character. The success of any organization will not reach beyond the character of its leaders. Excellence breeds character, and character breeds excellence. Demand excellence from your people,

> **Excellence breeds character, and character breeds excellence.**

and they will develop into people who also demand excellence of themselves and the people they lead.

IMPLEMENT THE LAW OF EFFECT

Educational psychologist E. L. Thorndyke did work in behavior modification around the turn of the century. It led him to discover what he called the Law of Effect. Simply stated, it is this: "Behaviors immediately rewarded increase in frequency; behaviors immediately punished decrease in frequency."

We must ask ourselves what is being rewarded in our organizations. Do we reward personal growth and development? If so, our people will be growing.

Several years ago I developed a list of behaviors and qualities that I expect from the people in my organization, and I determined to reward those behaviors. I call it the RISE program:

R *ewards*

I *ndicating*

S *taff*

E *xpectations*

In other words I decided to give rewards to staff members to indicate they were meeting or exceeding expectations. The qualities I value most highly and reward are a positive attitude, loyalty, personal growth, leadership reproduction, and creativity. Notice that personal growth is on the list. I want to encourage you to decide what you value, determine to reward it in your people, and put personal growth on your list. You will find that once you set up a positive reward system for achieving the right goals, your people will become their own best managers, and they will develop as leaders.

CARE ENOUGH TO CONFRONT

Rewarding the positive takes effort, but it is pretty easy to do. Confronting negative behavior is tougher. Many people avoid confrontation. Some fear being disliked and rejected. Others are afraid confrontation will make things worse by creating anger and resentment in the person they confront. But when a person's behavior is inappropriate, *avoiding confrontation always worsens the situation.*

First, the organization suffers because the person is not acting in its best interest. Second, you suffer because the person's deficiencies reduce your effectiveness. And finally, when a person is acting inappropriately and isn't told, you have robbed him of an important opportunity to learn and grow in his development process. Any time a leader avoids a confrontation, he should ask himself whether he is holding back for his own good or for the good of the organization. If it is for himself, he is acting under selfish motives.

Confrontation, in its best form, is a win-win situation. In this country we have been conditioned to believe that conflict always produces a winner and a loser. But that does not have to be true. To produce a win-win, we must approach confrontation with the right attitude. Think of confrontation as a chance to help and develop your people. And never confront in anger or out of a desire to show power. Do it with respect and the other person's best interest at heart. Here are ten guidelines I use to make sure I'm doing just that:

CONFRONT ASAP

The longer I wait, the less likely I am to do what must be done. Another benefit to confronting immediately is that I am not likely to have to argue with the person over details.

SEPARATE THE PERSON FROM THE WRONG ACTION

I am to address myself to the action and confront it, not the person. I must continue to support and encourage the person.

CONFRONT ONLY WHAT THE PERSON CAN CHANGE

If I ask a person to change something he can't, he will become frustrated and it will strain our relationship.

GIVE THE PERSON THE BENEFIT OF THE DOUBT

I always try to start from the assumption that people's motives are right and work from there. If I can give them the benefit of the doubt, I do—especially in areas that are open to interpretation or are unclear.

BE SPECIFIC

The person I'm confronting can only address and change what is specifically identified. If I can't identify specifics, I may be making some false assumptions.

AVOID SARCASM

Sarcasm indicates anger with people, not their actions. When confronting, I avoid sarcasm.

AVOID WORDS LIKE *ALWAYS* AND *NEVER*

When I tell a person never to do a certain behavior, I am asking him to cling blindly to a rule, even in situations when it's not the best thing to do. I'd rather encourage him to use his head and take the right course of action in any given situation, based on right principles.

TELL THE PERSON HOW YOU FEEL ABOUT WHAT WAS DONE WRONG

If the person's actions have offended me, I tell him right then and there. I don't want to be going back over old ground later in order to vent emotions.

GIVE THE PERSON A GAME PLAN TO FIX THE PROBLEM

I always want to help the person succeed, not fail. If I can help him fix the problem, everybody wins.

AFFIRM HIM OR HER AS A PERSON AND A FRIEND

I prepare to confront in the same way that I fix a sandwich. I put the confrontation in the middle like meat. On both sides I put affirmation and encouragement.

Positive confrontation is a sure sign that you care for a person and have his best interests at heart. Each time you build up your people and identify their problems, you give them an opportunity to grow.

> Positive confrontation is a sure sign that you care for a person.

MAKE THE HARD DECISIONS

In Chapter Two I pointed out that leaders must be willing to make difficult decisions in order to create a climate that encourages development. Some of those difficult decisions concern letting employees go. But there are hard decisions to be made during your leaders' development process too.

People respond differently to development, and I have found from personal experience that each person who does grow will plateau at one of six levels of development:

LEVEL 1. SOME GROWTH

Some people experience growth at a very slow rate and their growth lacks direction. These people improve almost imperceptibly. They may be competent, but they will never shine in their jobs.

LEVEL 2. GROWTH THAT MAKES THEM CAPABLE IN THEIR JOB

Many people mistakenly believe that simply doing their job well is the final goal in their development. It's not. Without a good developer or a strong desire for personal growth, many people stop here in the growth process.

LEVEL 3. GROWTH THAT MAKES THEM ABLE TO REPRODUCE THEMSELVES IN THEIR JOB

At this level of growth, people are beginning to add to their value because they are able to train others in their area of expertise. Some people who are technically strong but have marginal leadership skills are able to do this. Others with strong leadership skills can do it despite marginal technical abilities. People who are strong in both areas often move up to the next level.

LEVEL 4. GROWTH THAT TAKES THEM TO A HIGHER-LEVEL JOB

The jump from Level 3 to Level 4 is difficult. It requires that people are willing to dedicate themselves to growing both personally and professionally. As they are able to broaden their thinking and experience, they become more capable and valuable to their organization and leaders.

LEVEL 5. GROWTH THAT ALLOWS THEM TO TAKE OTHERS HIGHER

It is at this level that great leaders begin to emerge. These people are true developers of people, and they no longer add value to their leaders and organization—they *multiply* it.

LEVEL 6. GROWTH THAT ALLOWS THEM TO HANDLE ANY JOB

People who develop to this level are rare. If you have the privilege of helping people to this level, treat them with the greatest love and respect. These people are leaders who could make it anywhere. And they have skills and abilities that transcend any particular field or industry. In your lifetime if God blesses you with one or more of these people, together you will have the ability to make an impact far beyond your own individual capabilities.

Take a look at the figure on the next page. As you can see, the pool of people at each level is represented by a circle. The higher the level, the fewer people at that level. You will also notice that each successive jump gets more difficult as the levels get higher. Each takes more commitment, dedication, and tenacity than the one before.

The reason I write about hard decisions is that you will have to make hard decisions concerning every person you develop other than the person who makes it to Level 6. When you are a developer of people, you meet each person on the level where you find him, usually on Level 1, then you begin a journey. Your job is to walk alongside that person and help him for as long as he is willing to keep going and growing. When that person stops growing, that's when you have to do something difficult: You have to leave that person behind. Your relationship can continue, but your development of that person won't.

That is one of the difficult things about being a developer of people. We give people so much time, attention, and love that leaving one behind can be like letting go of one of our children. But you can't force a person to keep growing to the highest level. You have to make the hard decision of leaving that person on his own plateau. It's difficult, but it's a price worth paying in order to develop people.

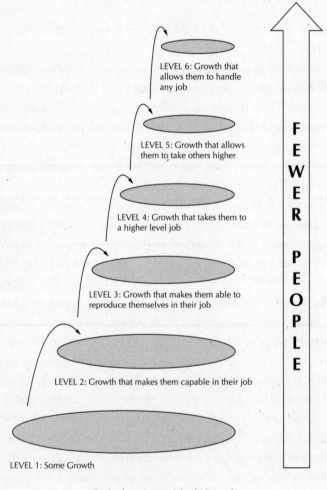

Pools of people at each level of growth

BE PERSONALLY SECURE

To be a great developer of people, you must be personally secure, because taking your people to the height of their potential may mean they will pass you by. As I mentioned in Chapter One, Andrew Carnegie wanted to be remembered as "a man who was wise enough to bring into his service men who knew more than he." It takes a very secure person to face that possibility, but without such a mind-set, you may be competing with your people instead of developing them.

As you prepare to lead and develop the people around you, I'd like you to keep in mind something Harvey Firestone said: "It is only as we develop others that we permanently succeed." All of the certificates of recognition we receive in life will fade. The monuments we build will crumble. The trophies will corrode. But what we do for others will make a lasting impact on our world.

SEVEN

THE LEADER'S HIGHEST RETURN:
FORMING A DREAM TEAM
OF LEADERS

Anyone who has ever experienced being on a team—from playing on a professional sports team to being a member of the junior high band—knows that being a part of a successful team can be one of the most rewarding experiences in life. And on the right team, it can also be one of the most powerful.

First, just what is a team? We know it's more than simply a group of people. If that's all it were, then people waiting at a trolley stop would make up a team. But they don't. I need to add that to be a team, a group must have a *common goal*, although that's not enough. Our people at the trolley stop have the common goal of waiting for the trolley car that will take them somewhere. Even if they had the same destination, it would help, but it would not be enough to make them a team. There must be *cooperation*, but once again, that doesn't complete the whole picture. Add *communication*—there is no team without communication.

Let's look again at our people waiting for the trolley to see how an ordinary group may act compared to a team. It's a hot, humid summer day. The group at the stop includes businesspeople in suits, mothers with toddlers and infants in strollers, construction workers, and homeless people. Finally, a crowded trolley pulls up to the stop. When everyone sees that the cars are packed, they all scramble. Each person runs to get a spot. A woman with a stroller does her best to herd her four children to the door of one of the cars, but she can't find a place with enough room to fit her whole family. By the time she tries another car, the doors close and the trolley moves away. She will have to wait thirty minutes for the next trolley.

The same trolley pulls into the next stop. Waiting is a team of twelve high school basketball players on a field trip with their coach. When they see how crowded the trolley cars are, they prepare to scramble too. One player shouts, "I'll check the first car to see if there's room." Another says, "I'll take the last one." The coach holds open the door to the full middle car because he knows that the trolley can't leave while a door is open. The player at the last car shouts, "There's room back here" as he holds that door open. Yet another player goes to find the teammate who went forward. As they reassemble in the last car, the coach counts to make sure everyone has made it.

As important as teamwork is, and as powerful as it can be to the success of an organization, many leaders don't teach their people how to work in teams. Management consultant Kenneth Blanchard observed:

> As I work in companies around the country, I often ask people what percent of their time do they spend in groups. Although managers report 60 to 90 percent of their time is usually spent in group activities, they also say they get little or no training in skills needed to work efficiently in groups. I know of few companies that focus training on this important skill.

Many leaders think that building a team and developing team-work is only for sports. They don't realize that they can build a team within their organization. Nor do they have any idea how to approach the task.

Developing leaders is wonderful: It's fulfilling and rewarding. But developing a team of leaders—that's incredible. A good team is always greater than the sum of its parts, but teams of *leaders* increase their effectiveness exponentially. With the right leaders teamed together, there is nothing they can't accomplish. Anyone who is developing leaders can also develop them into a team. It is the last development task that will yield the highest return.

THE QUALITIES OF A DREAM TEAM

In all my years of people development and team building, I have found that all successful teams share some common characteristics. If you, as the team leader or coach, can cultivate these qualities in your group of leaders, they will become a cohesive team capable of leaping tall buildings or performing any other required task. Here are those characteristics:

THE TEAM MEMBERS CARE FOR ONE ANOTHER

All great teams begin with this quality. It is the foundation upon which everything is built. Teams that don't bond can't build. Why? Because they never become a cohesive unit.

One of the best descriptions of this quality that I've ever come across was given by South Carolina football coach Lou Holtz. He said that he had once watched a television program that examined why men died for their country. In the program, which looked at United

States Marines, the French Foreign Legion, and the British Commandos, it was noted that men died for their country because of the love they had for their fellow man. In the show, they interviewed a soldier who had been wounded in combat and was recovering in a hospital when he heard his unit was going back out on a dangerous mission. The soldier escaped from the hospital and went with them, only to be wounded again. When asked why he did it, he said that after you work and live with people, you soon realize your survival depends on one another.

> **Teams that don't bond can't build.**

For a team to be successful, the teammates have to know they will look out for one another. When a team member cares about no one but himself, the whole team suffers. Uncaring people on a team remind me of a couple of guys in a story I once read: Two shipwrecked men sat together at one end of a lifeboat, doing nothing. As they watched intently, the people at the other end of the boat were bailing furiously. One man then said to the other, "Thank God that hole isn't in *our* end of the boat!"

I have found that one of the best ways to get members of a team to care about one another is to get them together outside of a work context in order to build relationships. Every year in our organization we plan retreats and other events that put our people together in social settings. And during those times, we also make sure they spend part of their time with staff members they don't know very well. That way they're not only building relationships, they're being prevented from developing cliques.

THE TEAM MEMBERS KNOW WHAT IS IMPORTANT

One of the things I enjoy most about a team experience is how the team functions as a single unit. All of its parts have a common goal and purpose. This quality is developed by making sure each team member knows what is important to the team. This quality, like the previous one, is foundational to team building. Without it team members cannot truly work together.

In a sport such as basketball, the players on a team recognize that scoring is what is important. When a team is more effective at scoring than the opponent, it wins. Because the team members know that, they spend their time improving and perfecting their ability to score. That is their focus. In contrast, in many organizational settings, the team members don't know what it means to "score." They may have a list of duties, but they don't know how those duties go together to make a score. It would be the equivalent of a basketball player who knew how to set a pick, dribble, pass, or toss up a ball, but who never knew all these skills were used together to score baskets. Without that knowledge, every time a player who was a good ball handler got the ball, he might dribble it until the shot clock ran out. That player could be the finest dribbler in all the world, and his ball handling could give spectators great joy. But the team would fail to score every time he touched the ball, and they would never win a game. On the other hand, if he knew dribbling was merely a tool used by a player so the team could score, then his attitude, actions, and effectiveness would change dramatically. And the whole team's success would follow in the wake of those changes.

You can see what happens if just one player on a basketball team doesn't know what is important to the team. It makes him ineffective. And when he is in the game, it is impossible for the team to succeed. The same is true in any organization. Anyone who doesn't know what's important to the team not only fails to contribute to the team, but actually *prevents the team from achieving success*. That is why it is so important for the leader of the team to identify what is important to the team and to communicate that information to her team members.

THE TEAM MEMBERS COMMUNICATE WITH ONE ANOTHER

The third foundational quality of an effective team is communication. Just as it is important for the team leader to communicate what is important to the team, the individual members of the team must communicate with one another. Without it, the players are likely to work against each other. Important tasks can be left undone, and team members can find themselves duplicating work.

Anyone who has played basketball is familiar with the situation in which two players go up for a rebound and fight one another for the ball, only to find that they are on the same team. On teams where players communicate with one another, a third player will shout, "Same team!" to make sure they don't lose the ball while trying to take it away from one another. That is what communication on the team is all about: letting each other know what's going on so the team's best interest is protected.

The same is true in nonsporting organizations. Clear and formal lines of communication must be established. But even more important, an atmosphere of positive communication must be established and encouraged on a daily basis. People on the team must be made to feel that they are in an environment where it is safe to offer suggestions or criticism without feeling threatened, freely trade information in the spirit of cooperation, and discuss ideas without being negatively criticized. Open communication among teammates increases productivity.

THE TEAM MEMBERS GROW TOGETHER

Once the members of the team care for one another, have a common goal, and communicate with one another, they are ready to start growing. Growth within a team is much like growth within a marriage. It is important and necessary. Without it, the team and its individual members do not improve. But like marriage, the growth should include shared experiences and periods of communication so team members stay connected to one another. In a marriage, when growth is not continuously interactive, eventually the two people's lives develop parallel but very separate courses. They cease to function together as a team. If much time passes, their two courses move farther and farther apart until neither one knows what the other is doing. Finally they won't care for each other, their goals will be different, and they will stop communicating. Their team is likely to fall apart.

In an organization, it is the team leader's responsibility to orchestrate the team's growth. He must make sure his people grow both personally and professionally. And he must ensure that their growth happens together—as a team.

When I work on growing my team members, I take several different approaches. First, we all learn together on a regular basis, at least once a month. In this way, I *know* there are some things everyone in the organization knows, and they share the common experience of learning these things together, regardless of their position or responsibilities.

Second, I regularly build small teams of learners. I periodically have groups of three or four work together on a project that requires them to learn. It builds strong relational bonds between those people. It's a good idea, by the way, to vary the members of these teams so that different people are learning to work together. It also gives you an idea about the particular chemistry of different groups as they work together.

Finally, I frequently send different people to conferences, workshops, and seminars. When they return, I ask them to teach others in the organization what they've learned. It gets everyone used to teaching and learning from each other. Shared experiences and the give-and-take of communication are the greatest ways to promote team growth.

THERE IS A TEAM FIT

As people who care about each other grow together and work toward a common goal, they get to know each other better. They start to appreciate each other's strengths and become aware of each other's weaknesses. They begin to recognize and appreciate each player's unique qualities. And that leads to the development of a team "fit."

The type of fit a team has depends on many things. It is more than just the way a group of people with particular talents come together. We have probably all seen teams made up of talented players at each position who should have been able to play well together but couldn't. Despite their talents, they didn't have the right chemistry.

> **A good team fit requires an attitude of partnership.**

A good team fit requires an attitude of partnership. Every team member must respect the other players. They must desire to contribute to the team, and they must come to expect a contribution from every other person. Above all, they must learn to trust each other. It is trust that makes it possible for them to rely on one another. It allows them to make up for each other's weaknesses instead of trying to exploit them. It enables one team member to say to the other, "You go ahead and do this task because you are better at it than I am," without shame or manipulation. Trust allows team members to begin working as a single unit, to begin accomplishing the things that together they recognize as important. Once the players know and trust one another, and develop a fit, the team's personality will begin to emerge.

THE TEAM MEMBERS PLACE THEIR INDIVIDUAL RIGHTS BENEATH THE BEST INTEREST OF THE TEAM

Once team members believe in the goals of their team and begin to develop genuine trust in one another, they will be in a position to demonstrate true teamwork. Their mutual trust will make it possible for them to place their own rights and privileges beneath the best interest of the team.

Notice that I mention the team members will be in a *position* to demonstrate true teamwork. That does not necessarily mean that they will. For there to be teamwork, several things must happen. First, they must genuinely believe that the value of the team's success is greater than the value of their own individual interests. They will be able to believe it only if they care about one another and if their leader has effectively cast the vision of what is important. Then they will recognize that their success will come with the team's success.

Second, for team members to place their individual rights beneath the team's best interest, personal sacrifice must be encouraged and then rewarded—by the team leader and the other members of the team. As this happens, the people will come to identify themselves more and more with the team. At that point they will recognize that individualism wins trophies, but teamwork wins pennants.

> **Individualism wins trophies, but teamwork wins pennants.**

EACH TEAM MEMBER PLAYS A SPECIAL ROLE

As the team fit becomes stronger and each person is willing to put the team first, people begin to recognize their different roles on the team. They can do this because they know what must be accomplished to win, and they know their teammates' capabilities. With that knowledge and some encouragement from the team leader, people will gladly assume appropriate roles. Philip Van Auken, in *The Well-Managed Ministry*, recognizes this as the *Niche Principle*. He says, "People who occupy a special place on the team feel special and perform in a special way. Team niches humanize teamwork."

In an ideal situation, each person's role is built on his or her greatest strengths. That way each person's talents can be maximized. But it doesn't always work exactly that way. Because the team's success is what is most important, sometimes the team members must be flexible. For example, anyone who follows professional basketball has heard of Magic Johnson. He played for the Los Angeles Lakers during the 1980s, when they were one of the best teams. His greatest talent was his ability to make plays happen, especially assists using incredible look-away passes. But Johnson was a player who was always willing to fill whatever role the team needed. Over several seasons, he started in NBA championship games as a guard, forward, and center. He may be the only professional basketball player who has ever done that.

The important thing is that all the team members take a role that fits the goals and needs of the organization as well as their own personal talents and abilities. When any role is not filled, the whole team suffers. The situation can be like the one in a story that management consultant James Lukaszewski told in one of his speeches:

> [One day a farmer] was sitting on his porch noticing a highway department truck pulling over on the shoulder of the road. A man got out, dug a sizeable hole in the ditch, and got back into the vehicle. A few minutes later, the other occupant of the truck got out, filled up the hole, tamped the dirt, and got back in the truck. Then they drove forward on the shoulder about fifty yards and repeated the process—digging, waiting, refilling. After a half-dozen repetitions, the farmer sauntered over to them. "What are you doing?" he asked.
>
> "We're on a highway beautification project," the driver said. "And the guy who plants the trees is home sick today."

As team leaders, we must recognize what roles need to be filled by our team members for the team to accomplish its goal. And when we see a role not being filled, we must make adjustments to the team to make sure the job gets done.

An Effective Team Has a Good Bench

In sports, the bench may be the most misunderstood resource of the team. Many "starting" players believe that they are important while the people on the bench are not. They believe they could do without them. Others who spend much of their time on the bench don't recognize their own contribution. Some mistakenly believe they don't have to bother preparing the way the starters do, that they don't have to be ready to play. But the truth is that a good bench is indispensable. Without a good bench, a team will never succeed.

The first thing a good bench gives is depth. In sports, many teams can produce a winning season. But when the level of competition goes up, such as in a play-off or a national tournament, a team without depth just can't make it. If the team does not have good reserve players, it will not be able to go the distance. I have yet to see a championship team that did not have a good bench. In fact, developing a good bench is what much of this book is about: selecting, equipping, and developing people to do their best and get the job done when they are needed.

Having a pool of good players able to play different roles gives the team leader great flexibility in any situation. In basketball, for instance, a coach will start a game with one group of people when playing against an opponent whose players are particularly tall. He may have another lineup when playing a particularly quick opponent. Some combinations of players will be great defensively. Others may be great at executing a run-and-gun offense. Which players he puts in the game will often depend on who his opponent is. Team leaders in other organizations will have the same kinds of options when they have a strong bench. With depth, the team can handle a variety of situations and demands with grace and effectiveness.

Another property of a team's bench is that it sets the tone for the whole team's level of play. This is true because the team's preparation depends on the bench. In sports, teams practice against their own players. If the starters practice only against weak players, their performance will not improve. But a good bench causes them to do their best all the time, to constantly improve. The same is true in any organization. If the level of play in the organization is high every day, then the team's performance will be top-notch when it really counts.

Finally, a good bench is a requirement for a successful team because it provides a place for a weary player to rest. On successful teams, when one of the players cannot make it any further due to fatigue or injury, his teammates carry the load and give him a rest. This is possibly the finest quality of teamwork—the willingness of one player to step up his level of play and go the extra mile for his teammate in a time of need. It is the ultimate indication of a player's desire to put the team and its goals first.

THE TEAM MEMBERS KNOW EXACTLY WHERE THE TEAM STANDS

In sports, the ability to know where their team stands at every moment during a game separates the great players from the adequate players. That quality, as much as talent, enables a player to move from one level of play up to the next, such as from college to the pros. Coaches have different terms for this quality. A football coach, for instance, might call it *football sense*. A basketball coach might call it *court sense* or *vision*. It is the ability to know how many seconds are left on the clock, how many points they are down, and which players are hot or hurt on each team. It is a quality that makes players, and therefore teams, great.

Outside of sports, the quality could be called *organizational sense*. It is the ability to know what is happening within the organization, how the organization stands in reference to its goals, how it stacks up against the competition, how the different players are doing, and how much more they can give in order to get the team where it needs to go. Not all team members are equally gifted with this sense. It is the job of the team leader to keep all of the

> **Knowing where their team stands at every moment separates the great players from the adequate players.**

players informed. He must get them to check on the team's progress and listen to the other players to know where the team stands. If all the team members are informed of where the team stands, they are in a better position to know what it is going to take for the team to succeed.

The Team Members Are Willing to Pay the Price

Time after time, success comes down to sacrifice—willingness to pay the price. The same is true of a winning team. Each member of the team must be willing to sacrifice time and energy to practice and prepare. He must be willing to be held accountable. He must be willing to sacrifice his own desires. He must be willing to give up part of himself for the team's success.

> **Success comes down to sacrifice— willingness to pay the price.**

It all comes down to the desire and dedication of the individuals on the team. It's as true in business as it is in sports. It's even true in war. In an interview with David Frost, General Norman Schwarzkopf, commander of the Allied forces in the Gulf War, was asked, "What's the greatest lesson you've learned out of all this?" He replied:

I think that there is one really fundamental military truth. And that's that you can add up the correlation of forces, you can look at the number of tanks, you can look at the number of airplanes, you can look at all these factors of military might and put them together. But unless the soldier on the ground, or the airman in the air, has the will to win, has the strength of character to go into battle, believes that his cause is just, and has the support of his country . . . all the rest of that stuff is irrelevant.

Without each person's conviction that the cause is worth the price, the battle will never be won, and the team will not succeed. There must be commitment.

When you build a team within your organization, you will be capable of a level of success you never thought possible. Teamwork for a worthwhile vision makes it possible for common people to attain uncommon results. And when the team members are not common people, but leaders, their accomplishments can multiply. All the team needs is the right coach. And becoming that coach is the subject of the next chapter.

EIGHT

THE LEADER'S GREATEST JOY:
COACHING A DREAM TEAM
OF LEADERS

In 1992 American sports journalists could talk about nothing but the Dream Team—the United States Olympic basketball team composed of Michael Jordan, Larry Bird, Magic Johnson, Charles Barkley, and other basketball greats. Some players on that team have been called the best ever to play the game of basketball. When people watched them play, the question was not whether they would win or lose. The question was, "What magnificent plays will I see, and how big a margin will the team win by?" The team was such an assembly of stars that even the players on the opposing teams were asking them for their autographs.

All coaches dream of having a team like that—players who know the game inside and out, who have the talent, the desire, and the discipline to compete and succeed on the highest level. Most leaders dream of the same thing, but most of them think it will never happen to them. And for many that's true—it won't. Why? Because they don't know what it means to be a winning coach.

Banker Walter Wriston, in *Harvard Business Review*, says, "The person who figures out how to harness the collective genius of the people in his or her organization is going to blow the competition away!" That is what a great leader does: He harnesses the collective genius of his team members. He knows how to select, motivate, and empower his people.

In over thirty years of leadership, I have been privileged to lead some wonderful teams of people. Through those years, I have discovered that in order to become a dream team coach, a leader must develop ten qualities.

THE QUALITIES OF A DREAM TEAM COACH

As Charles Frances once said, "You can buy a man's time, you can even buy his physical presence at a given place, but you cannot buy enthusiasm . . . you cannot buy loyalty . . . you cannot buy the devotion of hearts, minds, or souls. You must earn these." The following ten characteristics of a dream team coach are qualities that will earn a team's respect and loyalty, and they will motivate and empower the people to play like a dream team.

1. A DREAM TEAM COACH CHOOSES PLAYERS WELL

Throughout the book, I've given a lot of attention to identifying and selecting potential leaders. And you already know how to go about developing people into effective individual players. Choosing the right people is vital. Red Auerbach, longtime Boston Celtics president, said, "How you select people is more important than how you manage them once they're on the job. If you start with the right people, you won't have problems later on. If you hire the wrong people, for whatever reason, you're in serious trouble and all the revolutionary management techniques in the world won't bail you out." Another great sports leader, Lou Holtz, put it this way: "You've got to have great athletes to win. . . . You can't win without good athletes, but you can lose with them. This is where coaching makes the difference." Both men recognized that you have to begin with the right raw materials to create a winning team.

As Bobb Biehl says in *Increasing Your Leadership Confidence*, along with clear direction and sound finances, having the right players determines 60 to 80 percent of the success of any company or organization. If you want to give yourself a chance to win, start by picking winners.

> **Having the right players determines 60 to 80 percent of the success of any organization.**

I can identify what a winner looks like for my organization. I can tell whether a person has the potential to be an all-star contributor. I want the people close to me to:

Know my heart:	This takes time for both of us and desire on their part.
Be loyal to me:	They are an extension of me and my work.
Be trustworthy:	They must not abuse authority, power, or confidences.
Be discerning:	They make decisions for me.
Have a servant's heart:	They carry a heavy load because of my high demands.
Be a good thinker:	Our two heads are better than my one.
Be a finisher:	They take authority and carry out the vision.

> *Have a heart for God:*   My heart for God is my driving force in life.

When a person displays those qualities, I know he or she has the potential to play on my dream team.

2. A Dream Team Coach Constantly Communicates the Game Plan

Every good coach I've ever seen has worked from a game plan. He's got a plan not only for each individual game, but also for the development of the whole team over the course of the current and upcoming seasons. Once the game plan has been drawn up, he then communicates it to his team on an almost continual basis.

Bear Bryant, the late University of Alabama football coach, effectively communicated his game plan to his players. He recognized there were specific things his players needed to know. Five points explain what he believed a coach should do:

Tell them what you expect of them. This tells them how they are to fit into the game plan so they know what they should try to do.

Give them an opportunity to perform. This gives them a chance to be a part of the game plan, to carry out the vision.

Let them know how they're getting along. This lets them have an opportunity to learn, improve, and increase their contribution.

Instruct and empower them when they need it. This gives them the means to learn, improve, and increase their contribution.

Reward them according to their contribution. This gives them incentive for their effort.

The process must begin with communicating the game plan. That is the key to productivity. But it must continue with the exchange of information. Or as Sydney J. Harris said, information is giving out, while communication is getting through. When there is interactive communication between the team leader and his people, it empowers them to succeed.

3. A Dream Team Coach Takes the Time to Huddle

Another important part of the communication process is huddling. When a team huddles, it recalls the game plan and how it is to be implemented. When players don't take time to huddle, the results can be disastrous—or even comical.

The story is told of a gentleman who was walking down a residential street when he noticed a man struggling with a washing machine at the doorway of his house. When he volunteered to help, the homeowner was overjoyed, and the two men together began to work and struggle with the bulky appliance. After several minutes of fruitless effort, the two stopped and just looked at each other. They were on the verge of total exhaustion. Finally, when they caught their breath, the first man said to the homeowner: "We'll never get this washing machine in there!" To which the homeowner replied: "In? I'm trying to move it out!"

I find that things are never too busy or urgent to take the time to huddle. Here are five things that a huddle provides:

Focus. No matter how often or well a coach communicates the game plan, it never hurts to use huddle time to get people to refocus on what's important. In basketball, successful coaches take time-outs to huddle the players, especially when the opposing team is causing them to get out of their game plan. When they huddle, they go over the fundamentals to get back on track.

Even in politics focus is important. In 1992 following what analysts called flat campaigning by all the candidates, Bill Clinton was elected president. One reason was he was able to keep the campaign agenda focused on the areas where the American people most wanted change.

An opportunity to listen. When the team gets together, all the players and coaches have a chance to exchange information. Communication must flow both ways. When the coach is receiving the right information, it helps him send out the right information. New information can also prompt a coach to make adjustments.

An opportunity to make personnel changes. Sometimes the adjustments coaches need to make are changes in personnel or their responsibilities. Often the best way to solve a problem is to allow a different player to tackle it. A good coach can see that and is willing to make a change.

An opportunity to make play changes. Other times, the players are fine. What needs to be changed are the plays being run. Flexibility is a valuable quality in a coach. The best coaches are good at making necessary adjustments.

An opportunity to rest. Sometimes players just need an opportunity to stop, take a breather, and regroup. A well-timed huddle can help the team revitalize so they can carry on and succeed.

4. A DREAM TEAM COACH KNOWS WHAT HIS OR HER PLAYERS PREFER

Bringing out the best in team members requires that their coach know them and what is important to them. Padgett Thompson, a Kansas-based training organization, asked employees to rank their workplace wants in order of importance. They published those findings in *Training and Development Journal*. Of the many items they listed, the three things employees most valued were:

- Appreciation for a job well done

- A feeling that they're "in" on things

- Management understanding of their personal problems

Padgett Thompson then compared these results with the things supervisors *thought* employees would value. By comparison, the supervisors ranked these three items eighth, tenth, and ninth.

The supervisors' lack of knowledge concerning their employees may account for another survey statistic reported by John D. Hatfield and Richard C. Huseman in *Managing the Equity Factor*. It states that 85 percent of the workers across the United States said they could work harder on the job. More than half claimed they could double their effectiveness "if they wanted to."

The truth of the matter is that people don't produce because they aren't motivated or appreciated. Their leaders don't know what they want. People often change jobs for personal reasons, not for professional ones. And their emotions play the greatest part in their motivation. Good coaches know what their people prefer, and they use that knowledge to attain the team's and the individual player's goals.

5. A DREAM TEAM COACH EXCELS IN PROBLEM SOLVING

"A great leader doesn't treat problems as special," said Al Davis, successful owner of the Los Angeles Raiders. "He treats them as normal." Successful coaches never have "perfection" as their goal. If they did, they would fail every time. We live in an imperfect world where problems always occur. Certainly, a leader should strive for excellence, but he should expect problems to occur. And believe it or not, he should welcome them. Problems almost always create opportunities—to learn, grow, and improve.

All leaders can become good problem solvers. To do so, they must do four things: They must anticipate problems *before they occur*. They must maintain a positive attitude *while they occur*. They must use all their

> **Problems almost always create opportunities—to learn, grow, and improve.**

resources to solve them as quickly as possible so they *cease to occur*. And finally, they must learn from them so the same problems *do not occur again*.

Most issues requiring a coach's problem-solving skills fall into one of three categories. They are either player, preparation, or game issues:

Problem-solving issues with players. Issues with players require good communication skills as well as good problem-solving skills. One common problem is that the players don't work together as a team. (See Chapter Seven for ways to resolve this problem.) Another problem may involve players who are facing personal issues that require a coach's assistance and patient understanding. Possibly the most frustrating problem occurs when a player is not reaching his potential. A good coach must work with the player to help him identify his goals and then motivate him so that he begins to grow again.

Problem-solving issues with preparation. Probably the most common problem associated with preparation is the boredom factor. Many of the basics that must be taken care of in the preparation process can be boring. Good coaches provide a climate that minimizes boredom and reminds players of the positive results that preparation brings.

Related to the problem of boredom is morale. When morale is low, so is production. Good coaches keep their players' attitudes positive.

> **Good coaches approach each opponent from a fresh perspective.**

The last problem is a failure to prepare differently for different opponents (or projects). Good coaches approach each opponent from a fresh perspective and with creativity. If each new opponent is regarded as unique, success is more likely to come to the team.

Problem-solving issues with the game. As I discussed before, good coaches always approach the game with a game plan. That is a proactive approach. However, because problems do occur, good coaches also recognize that they may need to make reactionary decisions—decisions that should be made quickly then communicated clearly and immediately.

I once read that General Ulysses S. Grant kept a rather simpleminded soldier close to him at all times. When he prepared to give an order to one of his generals, he first gave the command to the common soldier to be sure he could understand it. In that way, he was sure all of his communication was clear and understandable.

Finally, all coaches recognize that their decisions will be criticized. No matter how the problem is solved, someone will say it was the wrong decision. A coach must learn to follow his convictions despite the roar of the crowds.

As you prepare for problems, keep in mind these words by Tom Landry, former head coach of the Dallas Cowboys. He said, "A successful leader has to be innovative. If you're not one step ahead of the crowd, you'll soon be a step behind everyone else." Approach problem solving creatively. And use all your people as resources. That's one of the reasons you've worked so hard to select and develop them.

6. A DREAM TEAM COACH PROVIDES THE SUPPORT NEEDED FOR SUCCESS

The greatest environment of support is created when coaches decide to be facilitators rather than dictators. The more the players and other coaches are involved, the more successful the team. Total control by the coach, even if he is somehow able to achieve it, is never as effective as a group effort. Look at the difference between how dictators and facilitators operate:

DICTATORS:

1. Hoard decisions.

2. Make decisions alone or restrict them to an elite group.

3. View truth and wisdom as their domain since they are the leaders.

4. Surprise their workers with edicts from above.

5. Guard their own interests.

6. Take for themselves.

FACILITATORS:

1. Push decisions down line.

2. Involve others as much as possible in key decisions and give people space to make those decisions.

3. View truth and wisdom as being accessible to everyone throughout the organization.

4. Let those responsible decide how the jobs will be done.

5. Serve everyone's interest by developing people.

6. Give to the organization.

In addition to providing an atmosphere of support in which everyone's participation is encouraged, great coaches also give their people plenty of affirmation. There isn't a player in the world who doesn't respond to it.

Another way the best coaches support their players is by simplifying the players' lives. Can you think of anyone who responds positively to bureaucratic red tape? I believe that:

Forms, Forms, Forms + Rules, Rules, Rules =
Frustration, Frustration, Frustration

If I can simplify, I do. I want to give my most creative and innovative people an open field to run in, not hoops to jump through.

Finally, one of the best ways to provide lasting support is by creating a winning tradition for the organization. Rookie professional players drafted by teams such as the Boston Celtics or Dallas Cowboys often speak admiringly of the team's tradition of winning. That tradition creates a positive atmosphere. It creates an invaluable momentum.

When a team gets a few wins under its belt, it creates a positive attitude and momentum. When it gets a few seasons of wins under its belt, it has a tradition. Then instead of the coach having to go out and find winners, winners come looking for him.

7. A Dream Team Coach Commands the Respect of the Players

Without respect, a coach will never be able to get his players to do what he asks. In *The Seven Habits of Highly Effective People*, Stephen Covey states it this way:

> If I try to use human influence strategies and tactics of how to get other people to do what I want, to work better, to be more motivated, to like me and each other—while my character is fundamentally flawed, marked by duplicity or insincerity—then, in the long run, I cannot be successful. My duplicity will breed distrust, and everything I do—even

using so-called good human relations techniques—will be perceived as manipulative.

It simply makes no difference how good the rhetoric is or even how good the intentions are; if there is little or no trust, there is no foundation for permanent success. Only basic goodness gives life to technique.

Respect must be earned over time. There are no shortcuts. It is earned through the consistent embodiment of three attributes:

> **Respect must be earned over time. There are no shortcuts.**

Trustworthiness. People never respect a person they cannot trust. Never. The best coaches know this and work immediately on letting their players know they can be trusted. Mike Krzyzewski, head basketball coach of Duke University, put it this way: "If you set up an atmosphere of communication and trust, it becomes a tradition. Older team members will establish your credibility with newer ones. Even if they don't like everything about you, they'll still say, 'He's trustworthy, committed to us as a team.'"

A caring attitude. In all my years of leading people, I must have said this more than a thousand times: "People don't care how much you know until they know how much you care." It's true. If players sense that you really care about them, that you have their interests at heart, they will listen to you and respect you. As former University of Michigan head football coach Bo Schembechler said, "Deep down, your players must know you care about them. This is the most important thing. I could never get away with what I do if the players felt I didn't care. They know, in the long run, I'm in their corner."

The ability to make hard decisions. Players cannot respect a coach who cannot make the hard decisions necessary for a team to succeed. When a coach is willing to make those decisions, the players know he is acting in the team's best interest. They feel secure, and they in turn are more likely to act in the team's best interest themselves. Tom Landry said, "Perhaps the toughest call for a coach is weighing what is best for an individual against what is best for the team. Keeping a player on the roster just because I liked him personally, or even because of his great contributions to the team in the past, when I felt someone else could do more for the team would be a disservice to the team's goals." He would also lose his players' respect.

8. A DREAM TEAM COACH DOES NOT TREAT EVERYONE THE SAME

One of the biggest mistakes a coach can make is to believe he must treat all of his players the same. Coaches are hired to win—not to make everyone happy or give everyone equal time, money, or resources. Every player must be given support and encouragement. But to believe that everyone must receive the same treatment is not only unrealistic but destructive. When all players are treated and compensated the same, poor or mediocre performance is being rewarded the same as outstanding contributions by the best players.

Great coaches give opportunities, resources, and playing time according to players' past performance. The greater the performer, the greater the opportunity. When you have a player like Michael Jordan, former Chicago Bulls great, you want to put the ball in his hands as often as possible.

There will be times you aren't sure about a player's performance level because you haven't had time to observe him. This is especially true when you have a rookie player. When that happens, give him frequent but small opportunities, and try to vary the

> **Give opportunities, resources, and playing time according to players' past performance.**

opportunities as much as possible. If you do, you will soon be able to determine his caliber of play. And that will show you how to respond.

9. A Dream Team Coach Continues to Win

There is only one challenge more difficult than winning that a successful coach faces: continuing to win. As tennis pro, golf pro, and former Olympic champion Althea Gibson said, "In sports, you simply aren't considered a real champion until you have defended your title successfully. Winning it once can be a fluke; winning it twice proves you are the best." Nearly anyone can point to a single victory they've had. But it takes more than one win to make a great coach. It takes continued positive performance.

Putting together successive winning seasons is so difficult in sports that teams bring in consultants such as psychologist Bruce Ogilvie to help them learn how to do it. In the July/August, 1988 issue of *Success* magazine, journalist Dan Gutman writes that Ogilvie suggests the following major points to ensure success:

Work on specific skills. No matter how many successes a team has had, there is room for improvement. There are people on the team who have not yet come close to fulfilling their potential. Work with each team member to foster improvement and growth. Focus each player on a new goal for the season.

Make a change. Every winner's temptation is to continue doing things exactly as before. But that is a flawed approach to success. You and your team will end up standing still, and another team will blow right past you. Use the momentum you've gained from past successes to continue to change and grow.

Reward the unrewarded. Every team has unsung heroes—people who were underappreciated for their contribution to the team's success. Find those people and reward them with praise, money, and further opportunities.

Transfer the burden. As I've said before, success always comes at a price. If your team has succeeded, it is because some members of the team have carried the burden by making sacrifices. They have given up time with their families, worked long hours, put their primary goals after the team's. Some people will have made such extensive sacrifices that they cannot continue to make them. Give them a break and transfer the burden to others who are willing and able.

Above all, don't dwell on yesterday's victory. If your focus is on what's behind you rather than what's ahead, you will crash. It's like the story I heard about salesman during the month of June. In the sales meeting held on July 1, the manger said, "I want to congratulate Kent on a job well done. He has sold more cars in a month than any other salesman." Everyone applauded. "But that was last month. Now let's focus on July." Celebrate victories, enjoy them briefly, and then look forward.

Another way to help players continue to win is to help them avoid burnout. The best way to do that is to see it coming and avoid it. Workplace psychologist Beverly Potter believes burnout can be prevented when it is caught in time. She suggests that a person look for lack of energy, sleeplessness, lack of creativity, inability to make decisions, chronic anger, bitter or sarcastic language, or physical symptoms such as exhaustion, tension headaches, body aches, and nausea.

John Madden, sports analyst and former championship coach of the Oakland Raiders, was a victim of burnout. He was once asked what the first signs of his burnout were. He said, "You won't have the energy because you won't have the interest. Suddenly, you don't care about the draft. You're not interested in minicamp. You don't care who the best college linebacker is. You don't care if they've signed any of your veteran players to contracts. When you don't care, it's time to go . . . you're history . . . you're done." Because he burned out, he was not able to continue coaching. The same can happen to you or your players. To continue winning, you've got to avoid burnout.

10: A DREAM TEAM COACH UNDERSTANDS THE LEVELS OF THE PLAYERS

One of the most common mistakes a coach can make is to misjudge the level of one of his players. If the leader doesn't work with each player according to where he is in his development, the player won't produce, succeed, and develop. According to management consultant Ken Blanchard, all team members fit into one of four categories with regard to the type of leadership they need.

Players who need direction: Players who need direction don't really know what to do or how to do it. At this stage in their development, you need to instruct them every step of the way. Anything these rookie players produce will be essentially what you do through them because they aren't capable of working independently.

Players who need coaching: At some point, a rookie starts being able to do more of the job on his own. He becomes more independent but still relies on you for direction and feedback. The two of you will be working in partnership.

Players who need support: At this level, the player is able to work without your direction. But he will still require your support and encouragement.

Players to whom you delegate: At this stage the player can be given a task, and you can be confident that it will be done. This player only needs you to lead. Provide vision on the front end and accountability on the back end, and the person will multiply your efforts toward success.

DELEGATION: THE DREAM TEAM COACH'S MOST POWERFUL TOOL

A leader may possess all ten of the previously mentioned characteristics, but if he does not learn the art of delegation, then he will never find himself coaching a dream team. Delegation is the most powerful tool leaders have; it increases their individual productivity as well as the productivity of their department or organization. Leaders who can't or won't delegate create a bottleneck to productivity.

The other benefit of delegation is that it increases the initiative of the people within the organization because it gives them a chance to grow and accustom themselves to succeeding.

If delegation is so important to a leader's success, why do some leaders fail to delegate effectively? There are many reasons:

> **Delegation is the most powerful tool leaders have.**

INSECURITY

Some leaders are afraid that if they're not in control of everything, it means they're not doing their job. They fear that others will criticize them for shirking their responsibilities. The bottom line is they are afraid that they will lose their job.

LACK OF CONFIDENCE IN OTHERS

Some leaders believe their employees are not competent enough to do the job, so they never delegate anything. They fail to realize that people grow into delegation by being given a chance to perform, make mistakes, and learn from them. To be successful, all leaders must eventually take the crucial step of allowing others to take part of the load. Leaders will make mistakes in delegation, and the people to whom they delegate will make mistakes. But that is when learning takes place.

LACK OF ABILITY TO TRAIN OTHERS

Successful delegators cannot simply dump tasks on their people without preparing them for the tasks. If they do, their people will fail and resent them. Instead, they must train their people both before delegating and afterward when mistakes have been made. When leaders learn to train others, they are better equipped to delegate.

PERSONAL ENJOYMENT OF THE TASK

It is difficult for people to give up tasks they love to perform. But sometimes giving up an enjoyable task is the best thing leaders can do. The question leaders must ask themselves is whether the task can be done by someone else. If so, it should probably be delegated. The leader should focus on performing tasks no one else can do, not simply on doing tasks he or she enjoys.

HABIT

Similar to enjoyment of a task is habit. Just because people master a task doesn't necessarily mean they should continue doing it. When a task becomes simple and straightforward, the leaders doing it should delegate it and move on to something more complex.

INABILITY TO FIND SOMEONE ELSE TO DO IT

Mark Twain once said, "Never learn to do anything. If you don't learn, you will always find someone else to do it for you." Although he wasn't serious, there is a kernel of truth in his statement. That truth is you must always be looking for people to whom you can give tasks. The times that people will track you down to ask you for something to do will be rare. A leader who can't find people to delegate to may not be looking hard enough.

RELUCTANCE CAUSED BY PAST FAILURES

As I mentioned, when leaders' early efforts to delegate fail, they sometimes become reluctant to delegate. As Ken Allen states in *The Effective Executive*, we should not try to rely solely on ourselves as a result of delegation failure, nor should we blame the people to whom we have given the task. "Rarely is delegation failure the subordinate's fault," he notes. "Maybe you picked the wrong person for the job, didn't train, develop or motivate sufficiently." If you have had trouble with delegation in the past, don't give up. Try to determine why the problem occurred, learn from it, and give delegation another try.

LACK OF TIME

Not having enough time to teach another person to do a job is probably the most common reason people give for not delegating. And not delegating is probably the most common reason people don't have enough time. Inability to delegate due to lack of time is short-term thinking. Time lost in delegating on the front end is recovered at the back end.

For example, let's say a leader takes an hour to perform a certain weekly task. He determines that to teach someone else to do that task, it will take him five hours initially, then an hour a week for the following three weeks. That totals eight hours of his time—*one whole day that he will lose* out of his busy schedule. He could continue to do the task himself for the next two months by devoting the same amount of time.

However, if he thinks long term, he realizes that by the end of the year, the eight-hour investment he makes will give him an additional forty-four hours of time to do other tasks. *That's one whole week of time he has gained!* And there is also the added advantage that the employee he has delegated to is better equipped to take on other tasks for him in the future. To break the vicious lack-of-time cycle, a leader needs the right person to delegate to and a willingness to put in the initial training time.

AN "I DO IT BEST" MIND-SET

Leaders who believe that to have something done right they have to do it themselves will end up accomplishing very little. The greatest problem new leaders have is their reluctance to move from *doing* the job to *managing* the job. Edgar Speer, chairman of U.S. Steel, said, "You don't even try to control how people do their jobs. There's no way to do that, furthermore, no purpose. Everyone does the job a different way, and they all want to show how well they can do it their way. The function of a supervisor is to analyze results rather than try to control how the job is done." If you want to do a few small things right, do them yourself. If you want to do great things and make a big impact, learn to delegate.

If you recognize yourself in any of the descriptions above, you probably aren't doing enough delegating. If you begin to miss deadlines, and crises become increasingly frequent, these may also be indications that you need to delegate tasks. And be on the lookout for employees under you who are ready to conquer new worlds—this is a prime time to delegate jobs to them.

STEPS TOWARD DELEGATION

Easing people into delegation is important. As I mentioned earlier, you can't simply dump tasks on people if you want them to succeed. I delegate according to the following steps:

Ask them to be fact finders only. It gives them a chance to get their feet wet and to become acquainted with the issues and objectives.

Ask them to make suggestions. This gets them thinking, and it gives you a chance to understand their thought processes.

Ask them to implement one of their recommendations, but only after you give your approval. This is a critical time. Set them up for success, not failure. And give lots of encouragement.

Ask them to take action on their own, but to report the results immediately. This will give them confidence, and you will still be in a position to perform damage control if necessary.

Give complete authority. This is the final step—what you've been working toward.

It is the job of a coach to make team members do what they don't want to do so they can become what they've always wanted to be. It can be done with the right tools and the right attitude. The more you work on your skills, the more you work on your own development; and the more you give of yourself to your players, the more successful you can become as a coach. If you truly give it all you've got, you, too, can someday coach a dream team. It will be one of the greatest joys of your life.

Here are two quizzes to help you gauge some of your coaching skills. The first one concerns delegation.

MISCONCEPTIONS ABOUT DELEGATION

QUESTIONS:
Answer each question as either True (T) or False (F).

1. Always delegate to the subordinate who has
   experience with similar tasks.   T   F

2. The person you delegate to should have as
   much information about the task as possible. T   F

3. Controls should be built into a delegated task
   from the beginning.   T   F

4. In delegated tasks, monitoring the method is
   as important as getting the desired results. T   F

5. The crucial decisions involved in a delegated
   task are still considered the territory of the
   delegator.   T   F

6. Always make the delegated task seem like a
   challenge even if it's drudgery.   T   F

7. Delegating means assigning work.   T   F

8. Don't offer advice when delegating.   T   F

9. Use the same procedures and systems of
   accountability with every subordinate when
   delegating to avoid favoritism.   T   F

10. If a subordinate fails in a delegated task, do
    not delegate to him or her again.   T   F

ANSWERS:

1. FALSE: If you repeatedly delegate similar tasks to the same
          people, they won't get additional opportunities
          to grow. It also shortchanges less experienced
          subordinates who need a chance to develop.

2. TRUE: The more background information you give the
          person who is about to do the task, the faster and
          easier the delegating process works. For more

experienced subordinates, you may be able to provide some information and then give them ideas on how to obtain additional information on their own.

3. TRUE: Controls not only help prevent disaster, they also give you the confidence to delegate.

4. FALSE: This is one of the most common pitfalls of an inexperienced delegator. Results are everything. Demanding that other people use your method can stifle initiative and creativity needed for successful delegation.

5. FALSE: This is another common mistake poor delegators make. With true delegation comes the right and responsibility to make decisions.

6. FALSE: Deceptive characterization of delegated tasks insults subordinates. And it erodes trust.

7. FALSE: True delegation includes handing over the rights and responsibilities to determine what work must be done, how it will be approached, and who will do it.

8. FALSE: Let people handle tasks their own way, but give them as much advice (and vision) as you think they need before they get started. Make yourself available to answer questions, but don't constantly peer over their shoulders or solve their problems for them. Learning to solve problems is part of the development process.

9. FALSE: Tasks are different, and so are people. The difficulty of the task as well as the experience and skill of the person must always be taken into

account. When you delegate, tailor the system of accountability to fit the delegatee.

10. FALSE: Don't give up on a subordinate because of a single failure. It might be due to circumstances beyond the person's control. The failure could even be a result of your method of delegation. Examine what went wrong and why.

SCORING:

Give yourself one point for each correct answer:

9–10	You're a top-notch delegator.
6–8	You know the fundamentals, but keep learning.
5 or less	You've uncovered a serious weakness in your leadership skills.

If you are currently responsible for leading or supervising people, you are responsible for their interaction as a team. This second test will help you determine how well you are doing as a coach:

HOW WELL ARE YOU COACHING YOUR TEAM?

Answer the questions using the following key; then total your score.

> 1 - Haven't thought about it yet
>
> 2 - Just in the early stages
>
> 3 - Solidly in progress
>
> 4 - Nearly accomplished
>
> 5 - Fully accomplished

1. I have chosen my players well.   1 2 3 4 5

2. I have proven to my players I care about them.   1 2 3 4 5

3. I have encouraged them to care about one another.   1 2 3 4 5

4. I know what my players prefer.   1 2 3 4 5

5. I actively encourage team growth.   1 2 3 4 5

6. I have developed a team that "fits."   1 2 3 4 5

7. I support my players.   1 2 3 4 5

8. I have taught them what is important.   1 2 3 4 5

9. I frequently show them the game plan.   1 2 3 4 5

10. I have modeled paying the price to them.   1 2 3 4 5

11. My players are willing to put the team   1 2 3 4 5
    before themselves.

12. I have developed a good bench.   1 2 3 4 5

13. I have encouraged each player to find   1 2 3 4 5
    and play his role.

14. I have my players' respect.   1 2 3 4 5

15. I reward my players according to their   1 2 3 4 5
    performance.

16. I have built a winning tradition.   1 2 3 4 5

17. I expect and prepare for problems.   1 2 3 4 5

18. I know the level of all my players.   1 2 3 4 5

19. I take the time to teach and delegate.   1 2 3 4 5

20. I do only the tasks that cannot be   1 2 3 4 5
    delegated.

SCORING:

90–100   You are a great coach with a dream team; you're
         ready for the championship.

80–89   You are an excellent coach; keep fine tuning your
         team and your skills.

70–79   You are a solid coach; don't' stop now; keep up the
         good work, and strive for the excellence that is
         within your reach.

60–69   Your players are beginning to look like a team;
         keep learning and building.

Below 60   You have a lot of work before you, but don't despair; use the principles in this chapter to begin team building and improving your coaching skills today.

NINE

THE LEADER'S FINEST HOUR: REALIZING VALUE TO AND FROM LEADERS

Alex Haley, the author of *Roots*, used to keep a picture in his office of a turtle sitting atop a fence. He kept it there to remind him of a lesson he had learned years before: "If you see a turtle on a fence post, you know he had some help." Haley remarked, "Anytime I start thinking, 'Wow, isn't this marvelous what I've done!' I look at that picture and remember how this turtle—me—got up on that post."

Both developed leaders and the people who developed them are like that turtle. They've gotten a lot of help. Their view from the fence post is made possible by others. Through the development process, the new leaders and the developers have value added to their lives.

Adding value to a person is much more than personal promotion or organizational improvement. It is true that people who have been developed get promoted. And it is equally true that organizations improve and expand when they have leaders devoted to the

> **People development is life-changing for everyone involved.**

development of others. But adding value is much more than that. It is the enrichment of people's quality of life. It is the expansion of their life purpose and capabilities. People development is life-changing for everyone involved. In *Bringing Out the Best in People*, Alan McGinnis said, "There is no more noble occupation in the world than to assist another human being." And as I noted in Chapter Four, Emerson said that we always benefit ourselves as well when we assist others.

VALUE ADDED TO NEW LEADERS

Several years ago when I was still leading a church as well as a business organization, I surveyed many of my leaders to illustrate the concept of adding and receiving value. I did that not necessarily because my organization offered the best examples, but because I knew them well. To examine what value I have added to leaders, I asked about ten people to give me some feedback. I requested, "Tell me about the value I add to you and the value I receive from you so that we can teach others what we do."

What follows is a summary of their responses. People said many kind things, but that is not the reason I am sharing their responses. I share them because I want to offer concrete examples showing that the development of people yields tangible results which can be recognized and later passed on to others. (In Chapter Ten I will share how some of these people are carrying on the development process with others around them.) After you spend time developing your people, you will find that they will respond in the same way that mine do.

MODELING

Most of the leaders in my organization identified modeling as something important that I do for them. One person said, "You set the pace of the organization. You never ask for more than you are willing to give yourself. This 'watermark' provides continual motivation for me to give my best." Modeling is an important motivator because it shows people not only what you expect, but what can be accomplished.

One of the most important things that my people said I model is a dedication to continue growing personally. When they see it in me, they recognize its importance. And they soon adopt that belief as their own. Even if they leave me tomorrow, they will continue to grow because they now recognize that belief as their own.

VISION AND DIRECTION

The leader of every successful organization casts vision for his or her people. I have always made sure that the people around me know my vision, because without that focus we cannot accomplish our goals. A staff member observed, "His ability to keep focused on the big picture . . . keeps me from having tunnel vision." Said another, "He provides vision and direction. By keeping in touch with him, I know that I am staying on target with my professional focus." Burt Nanus, in *Visionary Leadership*, wrote, "There is no more powerful engine driving an organization toward excellence and long-range success than an attractive, worthwhile, and achievable vision of the future, widely shared."

Having and sharing a vision does even more than drive an organization. It also gives people vision and direction for their individual lives. As they contribute to the larger goals of the organization, they begin to identify more clearly a vision for themselves. As that vision becomes clearer and that sense of direction stronger, their lives become more meaningful.

ENCOURAGEMENT AND AFFIRMATION

Everyone I surveyed said that they felt encouraged by me. That delights me because I want more than anything else to let my people know that I love them and want the best for them. One person said,

"He gives me personal encouragement and affirmation. He's the best I have ever seen at this in my life. Almost to a fault . . . Sometimes I run into people who are not doing something real well [but] their opinion is that John loves them." Another said, "He cares about me personally, and I believe he has my best interests at heart. He wants me to win. His positive attitude and encouragement let me know that he is happy when I succeed. He cares about what is most important to me—my family."

People in our society are underencouraged. They desire encouragement desperately but get it infrequently. There are two main reasons why the people in my organization feel very encouraged. First, I have spent time getting to know them and developing relationships with them. I know who they are, where they've come from, who their spouse is, who their children are. I know their gifts and their goals. I really know them. Second, I love them, and I express that love to them on a regular basis. I'm not talking about simply praising them for the work they do. I let them know that I care about them and love them as people first. There is no substitute for a relational foundation with people. You must have that to build upon if you are going to develop people. Even if you do nothing more than get to know your people and love and accept them, you will have added value to their lives.

BELIEF IN THEMSELVES

Most of the people I have spent my time developing are not shrinking violets. Even before they met me, they were not timid. Yet even people who already have confidence can be encouraged to believe more strongly in themselves. One staff member wrote, "John will often drop by my office to see how I am doing, to affirm me, to tell me once again how much he appreciates the load I carry. From the beginning, he encouraged me to do anything I dreamed. He encouraged me . . . to take on projects that I've never tackled before, and to always keep growing."

One of the ideas I examine in detail in my book *The Winning Attitude* is that it is impossible for people to perform consistently in a manner inconsistent with the way they see themselves. This is true no matter what positive or negative circumstances people face.

> **Believe in people, and they will rise to fulfill that belief.**

People who believe that they can succeed do so even when repeatedly dealt adversity. Others can be given the best of everything in life and still fail because they see themselves as failures.

When I know the leaders in my organization, believe in them, encourage them, and help them to succeed, it helps to strengthen their belief in themselves. I try to help them win increasingly larger victories. People almost always rise to meet your level of expectations. Believe in them, and they will rise to fulfill that belief.

WILLINGNESS TO TRY NEW THINGS

"He gives me confidence to risk and thereby reach new heights. And all the while he has a sincere positive belief in me," one of my leaders said. One of the most important results of people's belief in themselves is their willingness to try new things. When people do only what is comfortable for them, they get into a rut. They stop growing. But by being willing to take risks, people perform tasks they thought were impossible. They achieve more than they thought they could and become more than they thought they were. The kind of growth that comes with risk adds incredible value to people's lives.

PERSONAL DEVELOPMENT

Time w/ others

I have made it a practice to set aside time to develop those around me. One leader said, "You have purposefully mentored and coached me now for more than a decade." I give my leaders time for counsel and advice. I help them wrestle with difficult situations. I also schedule time for equipping them on a regular basis. Several leaders cited the monthly leadership instruction that I give as being valuable. Another reminded me of the experiences I've shared. She said, "He always wants the people around him to be able to experience with him the privileges and opportunities he has been given."

I try to give my people what I can. Sometimes it is time with them. At other times I am able to give guidance. If I can share a valuable experience, I do. As an example, that same staff member mentioned how with my help she was able to have breakfast in Korea with Dr. Cho, pastor of the largest church in the world. Another one of my staff members had always dreamed of meeting Billy Graham in person. When I had an opportunity to meet with the great evangelist, I shared that experience with that staff member by taking him with me. These two incidents were exciting to my staff members, but they were no more valuable then the more common growing experiences that I try to share with them day to day. I look for opportunities to share myself with my people, and you should too.

> **Look for opportunities to share yourself with people.**

COMMITMENT TO PERSONAL GROWTH

By now you know how important personal growth is to a person's success. It is what adds the greatest value to a person's life. Here is what one leader in my organization said about it:

> John is committed to growth, both personally and corporately, no matter what the cost. Because he lives on the edge, always desiring growth and challenge in his life, he gives me energy, motivation, and courage to make the tough decisions and never to become satisfied. John has had to fire people, say no to people, and prioritize his life in order to keep growing. He is willing to pay the price of loneliness as a leader!

As she indicated, I'm not the only one in my organization paying the price of personal growth. All of the top leaders around me are dedicated to it, day in and day out. If I were to leave the organization tomorrow, they would continue to pay the price necessary to keep growing. And as Walter Lippman said, "The final test of a leader is that he leaves behind in other people the convictions and will to carry on."

EMPOWERMENT

I have found that people become empowered when you provide them with three things: opportunity, freedom, and security. I give my leaders opportunities to do new things for the organization, the freedom to accomplish those things using creativity and initiative, and the security of knowing I will back them up, even when everything doesn't go as planned. Said one staff member, "You have assured me that you will do anything in your power to help me, which provides me a sense of security and trust." I love to see the people in my organization succeed, and empowering them makes that possible.

> People become empowered when you provide them with three things: opportunity, freedom, and security.

Empowerment can be a tricky thing to give. You have to balance your own needs with the empowered leader's development while always keeping in mind the best interests of the organization. One of the leaders in my organization identified this as the "rope principle":

John is constantly giving me enough rope to allow me to get the job done myself, but not so much that I hang myself . . . He also balances the development of the person with the good of the organization using the "rope principle." He will wait a little longer than he prefers to get something accomplished if the staff member will be developed in the process, but he will never let the rope go so long as to hurt the organization as a whole.

One of the leaders I surveyed identified empowerment as the characteristic that adds the greatest value to leaders. He said:

Motivation, believing in, mentoring, and all the other traits tap into what is inside the person. Empowerment adds a new dimension to the person that did not and often cannot exist or come into existence on its own . . . There is a great responsibility with the gift of empowerment. With the wrong motives a leader can empower for his/her own good rather than for the good of the people and the organization. John has always put the organization and individual people before himself.

Adding that new dimension to a person in your organization will not only make him a more powerful leader, it will also enable him to receive the value of the next item on the list.

BEING A PART OF SOMETHING GREATER THAN THEMSELVES

> To live a worthwhile, meaningful life, a person must be a part of something greater than himself.

To live a worthwhile, meaningful life, a person must be a part of something greater than himself. I challenge the people around me to live a life that has not temporal, but eternal, impact. I want each member of my staff to become the person he was created to be—to reach his potential.

One of the most encouraging comments in the survey came from one of the people closest to me at INJOY. He said, "He allows me to accomplish greater things with him than I could alone." That is one of the greatest rewards of adding value to people's lives. It comes back to you multiplied.

VALUE ADDED TO ME BY THE PEOPLE I HAVE DEVELOPED

If I were only able to add value to my people and receive nothing in return, I would still do it. But that's not how it works. No matter how much I give, I always receive more in return. It's absolutely incredible.

> One of the greatest rewards of adding value to people is that it comes back to you multiplied.

In my years as an organizational leader, I have found that all employees are one of two types: salary takers or salary makers. The takers give as little as possible and take their salary. The makers give everything they've got and make a contribution beyond the salary they earn. I have found that people who are willing to be developed are always salary makers. You can see the difference between the two types of people by the things they say:

SALARY TAKERS	SALARY MAKERS
What will I receive?	What can I give?
What will it take to get by?	I'll do whatever it takes to get it right.
It's not my job.	Whatever the job, I can help you.
Someone else is responsible.	I'm responsible.
How can I look good?	How can the team look good?
Will it pass?	Is it my best?
The paycheck is the reason I work.	The paycheck is a by-product of my work.

| Am I better off because I work here? | Is the team better off because I work here? |
| Pay me now, I'll produce later. | I'll produce now. You can pay me later. |

Here are the specific ways the leaders in my organization add value to me. This list consists of the items of value they identified in response to a memo I sent them. I added "Balance of Gifts." It is an added value important to me that they did not specifically identify.

LOYALTY

Many of the leaders in my organization identified loyalty—to me and to the organization—as a characteristic of the esteem they feel for me. One person joked, "I might not walk off a cliff for him, but I would certainly consider it!" Others mentioned their desire to protect the interests of the organization because they believe in it, or the desire to protect me from minor pressures that I don't need to handle myself. I am grateful for all of these things.

I also recognize the loyalty of my leaders comes from their belief in what the organization is doing and their sense of commitment to the team. The people around me work beautifully together. They always seem ready to jump in and do whatever they can. They put their own personal interests beneath the best interests of the team.

ENCOURAGEMENT

Encouraging others makes them want to encourage you too. One of my leaders wrote, "I make it a point to continually encourage John. I believe we all need encouragement from time to time. He is a great model in this area, and I take great joy in reciprocity."

I am naturally a very positive person, so I don't get down in the dumps. But my schedule is often very demanding, and I do get tired. When that happens, my staff is always there for me. Not only do they encourage me, they also offer to help carry the load in any way they can.

PERSONAL COUNSEL AND SUPPORT

A valuable result of developing leaders is the advice and counsel you can receive from them. I benefit from the knowledge and wisdom of the leaders in my organization. One of them said, "I am able to confront and share with John what I think or feel, even when I know he may disagree. I'm not a yes-person." I enjoy hearing the perspective of another leader. And I respect honesty. In fact, the opinion of a person who doesn't agree with me often teaches me more than the perspective of someone who agrees. Another leader said, "I believe that John knows that I am always prepared to provide input to him in any area he requests and desires. He also hopefully knows that he can count on me for 100 percent support." I appreciate the support and advice I get from my people. It adds incredibly to my life.

FOLLOW-THROUGH

I have a great group of people around me that I call "door closers." I call them that because I can hand off a task or project to them and know that they will follow through with it to the very end and close the door behind them. They implement ideas, complete projects, handle details, and perform problem solving for me. They also create and implement their own ideas within the context of the vision I cast. They are constantly furthering the goals of the organization. As one of them said, "I free you up for more important work. I carry part of the load."

The work these leaders do is very important to me and the organization. It must be done, and it is something they can do effectively. Each time I am faced with a new task, project, or activity, I always ask myself, "Is there someone else in the organization who can do this effectively?" If there is, I delegate it. I allow someone else to do the follow-through. That, in turn, leads to the next valuable thing that the people around me give to me.

TIME

I have many highly skilled, effective leaders working in my organization. Partly due to the time I have spent developing them, there are few things that they can't do for me and the organization. That allows me more time to do the things that only I can do or that others cannot do as well. As one person in my organization said, "I free him up to do what he does best: teach, lead, preach, motivate, etc." Time is an incredible gift to receive. The people around me free me from being a slave to the urgent so that I can accomplish the important.

BALANCE OF GIFTS

Like all people, I have strengths and weaknesses. Some of my areas of weakness I have been able to improve through personal growth and development. There are other areas where I have much room for improvement, especially in areas that go against my temperament. The people around me add value to me by balancing out my deficiencies with their gifts.

I was born with a sanguine choleric temperament—emphasis on choleric.[1] I enjoy making things happen. And I'm always moving forward. Stopping to reflect on what I've done in the past is not one of my strengths. For example, when I was a pastor at Skyline Wesleyan Church there were times when I would teach principles in a sermon that I later could teach to others outside the church or include in one of the lessons that I sent out to leaders each month through INJOY. But once I finished the last Sunday service, I wouldn't think about it again. That was a weakness.

Fortunately, the people I've developed help me to round out those areas of weakness. In the case of my sermons, for over ten years I had an assistant who would ask me questions each Monday to make me reflect on what I'd taught. Then she made notes on my comments and filed them away for my future use in other lessons.

ATTRACTION OF OTHERS

For an organization to continue building and growing, it must continually attract new people of high quality. In Chapter Three I shared with you that it is important to have leaders identify and recruit potential leaders. As important as that is, I can't give it as much time as I'd like. But the leaders in my organization do. They are constantly raising up new leaders. Unlike many people who head organizations, I have been fortunate never to find myself in a place where I had positions of leadership to be filled and no people to fill them.

PEOPLE DEVELOPMENT

Every leader I surveyed listed the development of other people as one of their top priorities and as a way they add value to me. They know that the development of leaders adds more value than anything else they do. Of people development, one leader wrote, "This is my passion. To select, equip, and develop people to love God, and to love and lead people." Another leader said, "I give depth to his leadership organization through discipling others and passing on to others what he has done for me, i.e., providing an environment for growth." And their development of people is focused not just on others around them, but also on themselves. They continue to be committed to their own personal growth. As one leader commented,

"I work on maintaining personal integrity and the development of my character for the sake of the organization and its influence." And what he does in his own development continues to make a positive impact on everyone in his sphere of influence, including me.

INCREASED INFLUENCE

Truly the bottom line on developing the leaders around you is that it increases your influence. In *Developing the Leader Within You*, I give what I consider to the be the greatest definition of leadership: *Leadership is influence.* One of the leaders I surveyed said, "I represent you to the masses that you cannot touch on a regular basis due to sheer time and numbers." For example, back at Skyline, the church I led, attendance on a busy Sunday was close to 4,000 people. If I wanted to touch each of those people personally by meeting with them for just thirty minutes, in addition to all of my other responsibilities, I would have had to meet with more than ten people every day for about six hours, seven days a week, for fifty-two weeks without missing a single person or taking a single day off. At the end of a year, I would have met with everyone who had attended Skyline on *one* Sunday. No one could keep up that kind of pace.

But even though I couldn't personally meet with every one of those people, I could still influence them—through my team of leaders. Each of them reached out and touched hundreds of lives. And each of them developed a team of leaders who, in turn, reached out and touched others' lives. As I continued to grow personally and develop others, my influence continued to grow. By the end of my life, if God grants me the productive life I anticipate, I will have positively influenced over ten million people—not just by myself alone, but through the leaders I have developed around me. As one of the top leaders in INJOY said, "I afford him the opportunity to increase his influence way beyond what he could do by himself single-handedly."

When you develop leaders rather than followers, they will do the same for you. And they will carry on the tradition just as some of my leaders have. The final chapter of this book describes how four of the leaders I developed have become first-rate developers of leaders in their own right.

TEN

THE LEADER'S LASTING CONTRIBUTION: REPRODUCING GENERATIONS OF LEADERS

It is time for a new generation of leadership," John F. Kennedy said in a television address during his 1960 campaign for the White House. Perhaps no president realized the need for successive generations of leaders more than Kennedy, the first commander-in-chief born in the twentieth century. He emerged as the nation's leader on the brink of a decade filled with radical changes.

As I explain in *Developing the Leader Within You*, most people believe that each new generation of leaders is born rather than developed. They think that new leaders come out of the womb as leaders and simply wait until they are old enough to take their rightful places in society. As a result, many leaders are willing simply to produce followers, expecting new leaders to show up on the scene when their time comes. Those types of leaders have no idea how much they are limiting their own potential and the potential of the people around them.

As I have said before, a leader who produces followers limits his success to what his direct, personal influence touches. His success ends when he can no longer lead. On the other hand, a leader who produces other leaders multiplies his influence, and he and his people have a future. His organization continues to build and grow even if he is personally unable to carry on his leadership role.

As a leader you may have followed all the guidelines in this book. You've created the right climate and identified potential leaders. You've nurtured, equipped, and developed them. You've built a great team and learned to coach them. At this point, you may think your

> **A leader who produces other leaders multiplies his influence.**

job is done. It's not. There is one more crucial element, and it is the true test of success for a leader who develops other leaders. The leaders you've developed must carry on the tradition of development and produce a third generation of leaders. If they don't the building process stops with them. True success comes only when every generation continues to develop the next generation, teaching them the value and the method of developing the next group of leaders.

> **True success comes only when every generation continues to develop the next generation.**

I have spent the greater part of my life developing leaders who are in turn producing another generation of leaders. And by the way, the new generation of leaders they are developing includes many people chronologically older than they. In fact, up until a few years ago, the majority of people I spent my time developing were older than I am. I was called to begin dedicating myself to the process of developing leaders around me when I was still in my twenties.

TRAITS OF A POTENTIAL LEADER

Many leaders make the mistake of believing that they can only develop people like themselves—in personality, temperament, natural abilities, and socioeconomic background. But that is not true. Leaders can develop many kinds of people. When I was a pastor at Skyline there were four people I considered to be my greatest successes in leadership development, and what was required for their development was very different in each case. Yet they were developed, and they added incredible value to my life—at that time, more than anyone else outside of my family. Each person not only lightened my load and extended my influence, but they were especially successful at carrying on the tradition of developing leaders around them.

Each of the four people presented a different challenge to me as a developer of leaders. They had very different levels of experience. Their temperaments were different from mine and from each others'. Some had well-developed relational skills, while others didn't. But despite their differences, they all were capable of becoming leaders and of developing other leaders. I have found that there are three things that are required for a person to become a leader:

DESIRE

The ability to become a leader begins with desire. It is the only thing that the developer cannot supply. The amount of desire will largely determine the potential leader's progress. Great desire can overcome a multitude of natural deficiencies in a leader.

RELATIONAL SKILLS

In all my life, I have never met a great leader who did not possess good relational skills. They are the most important abilities in leadership. Without them, a person cannot lead effectively. Many people believe that relational skills are determined at birth and cannot be learned. But that's not true. People's

> **Relational skills are the most important abilities in leadership.**

temperaments incline them to relate to others in a particular way, but they do not dictate their relational abilities. Even the most introspective, melancholic person can learn to develop good relational skills. For nearly everyone, relational skills can be learned and improved.

PRACTICAL LEADERSHIP SKILLS

These are the "how tos" of leadership that a person acquires through your modeling, equipping, and developing. These, too, are learned.

When I came into contact with each of the four leaders I will introduce to you, they all had different skills, but they had in common great desire.

A FOLLOWER BECOMES A LEADER

Barbara Brumagin, who was my personal assistant for eleven years, came to me as a highly competent secretary. She worked hard, and she had a wonderful servant's heart, but she did not lead others. It wasn't a natural part of her personality, nor was she well equipped to lead. She had always been a follower, but I could see that she had great potential. And even more important, she had great desire.

When I first came to Skyline Church, I began looking for an assistant, and Barbara was recommended to me by one of the pastors on staff. When we met to discuss the position and I began asking her questions, she was uncommunicative almost to the point of being rude. I quickly changed tacks and began doing the talking: showing her my goals and vision for the church, myself, and her. After listening for a few minutes, she began communicating with me. I immediately saw that she would be perfect for the position, and I hired her. I found out later that she had come to the interview against her will because she had envisioned being a secretary in a church as boring and devoid of growth opportunities. She was more interested in learning and growing, and grow she did. Barbara was like a sponge.

With Barbara's development, I went slowly. It took her about two years before she felt really confident in her position and began showing signs of leadership. I modeled leadership, exposed her to teaching, and worked interactively with her. I was always careful to spend time explaining not only what things I wanted her to do but also why I wanted her to do those things. She once told me that she felt like she was getting personally developed every day. After we had worked together for a few years, she knew me so well that she could answer any question for me or make nearly any decision in the same way I would. In fact, she and I once took a personality test. I answered each question, and then she took the same test and answered the questions as *she thought I would*. When we compared answers, she had only missed two questions. She was quick to point out that she had missed one of those because I had answered it wrong—and she was right!

You may have people you are preparing to develop who are non-leaders like Barbara was. If you do, there are four things to keep in mind as you develop them:

Maintain a Positive Environment

People who do not already possess leadership skills must have an environment that is positive and conducive to their growth. Without that environment, they will be afraid of growth. With it, they will be willing to learn and try new things. Provide the environment; then keep them close to you so that they can begin learning how you think.

Express High Belief in Them

People who are not naturally inclined toward leadership and who have no leadership experience often get discouraged easily. Because they have not been leaders before, they will make mistakes.

They may make a lot of them, especially in the beginning. Their development is likely to be a long process. By expressing a high belief in them, you encourage them to persevere, even when things get tough.

Empower Them

In the beginning, followers are reluctant to assume leadership roles, so they must be empowered by their leaders. Start by walking alongside of them and giving them authority in your name. As time goes by, others will begin to reframe their view of the new leaders, and the new leaders' view of themselves will also change. Eventually, people will begin recognizing them for their own authority.

Play to Their Strengths

It is critical that you begin the development process by playing to their strengths. Because they have experienced few successes in leadership before, they need a few wins under their belts. It really accelerates the development process, and the new leader begins building momentum.

When you begin developing a follower into a leader, the time and energy required will slow down your progress. You may be tempted to stop developing the person, but don't. It could be a terrible mistake. In the case of Barbara, developing her took a little bit of time in the beginning, but not only did she more than make up for it by giving me eleven wonderful years of service, she is now passing on what she has learned to others.

A MANAGER BECOMES A LEADER

When I first met Dan Reiland and his wife Patti at a leadership conference I was holding in Indiana, he was still a seminary student. Dan had been a member of Skyline, felt the call to ministry, and gone to seminary before I became Skyline's senior pastor. He then returned as an intern during my first year at the church.

Dan's development was very interesting. Dan's smart, he's a good scholar, and he was a good student in seminary. He had often been put in charge of the activities he was involved in, and he had even been the president of his class. But despite his good qualities, he wasn't a leader. He was really more of a manager.

Managers think differently from leaders. Managers tend to focus on tasks and systems. They have narrow vision, and they sometimes tend to be dogmatic. And most of all, their focus is not relational. Dan tended to focus on tasks and the work at hand. He was a hard worker, but he put tasks ahead of people. I remember one day several of us were talking in an office hallway, and Dan walked right through us without saying a word. It was at that point that I knew he and I needed to have a serious conversation, or he wasn't going to make it on my team.

I was able to sit down with Dan and confront him about his relational skills, because he knew that I believed in him and genuinely cared about him. Ironically, I found out that Dan really loved people, and in his heart, he wanted to relate to them. But his internal desire wasn't made clear by his actions. People working with him had no idea how much they mattered to him. It was then that I began spending extra time with him developing his skills to relate to others as a leader does. I taught him to walk slowly through a crowd, interacting with people rather than going past them in order to accomplish tasks. Now, as I mentioned in Chapter Three, he became the executive pastor of Skyline and was invaluable to me. His ability to relate to others has become one of his strongest qualities, and he considers it foundational to his ability to lead.

> **How big
> we think
> determines
> the size of our
> accomplishments.**

If you have potential leaders who think like managers, your goals are to help them develop better relational skills and change their pattern of thinking. While you have to *slow down* to teach a follower how to lead, you may have to come to a *complete stop* in order to help a manager become a leader. The reason is that you will sometimes need to stop what you're doing, walk the person through your thought process, and then explain why you're doing what you're doing. You must constantly show them the big picture until they begin to see it for themselves.

I have found that all true leaders share some common characteristics in their thinking.

LEADERS THINK BIG

They always look at the big picture, and they know that their success is only as great as their goals. As David Schwartz said, "Where success is concerned, people are not measured in inches, or pounds, or college degrees, or family background; they are measured by the size of their thinking. How big we think determines the size of our accomplishments." If you consistently show the people you are developing the big picture and keep stressing possibilities rather than problems, they will start thinking big.

LEADERS THINK IN TERMS OF OTHER PEOPLE

Leaders don't focus on themselves and their own individual success. They think about the success of the organization and other people. They have an other-people mind-set. To develop others, you must teach them to think in terms of how they can promote others, develop others, take along others.

LEADERS THINK CONTINUALLY

People who are not leaders are content to sit back and allow others to do the thinking. Leaders are constantly entertaining new ideas, considering new resources, thinking about improving, contemplating finances, managing their time. Thinking continually enables leaders to keep stretching themselves and growing their organizations. As you develop leaders, model this kind of thinking, and promote it by asking questions.

LEADERS THINK BOTTOM LINE

While others get bogged down in the details, leaders look for the bottom line. If you often ask the people you are developing to give you the bottom line, they will soon begin determining what it is before you ask for it. Eventually they will begin thinking in those terms un-prompted.

LEADERS THINK WITHOUT LINES

People who are not leaders automatically gravitate toward lines—limitations set by others. Maybe people are taught this in kindergarten when they are instructed to stay within the lines while coloring. But leaders are more creative than that. They look for options and opportunities. They try to take things in a new direction, or beyond the limit. Progress and innovation are made by people who think without lines.

> **Progress and innovation are made by people who think without lines.**

LEADERS THINK IN TERMS OF INTANGIBLES

Leaders are abstract thinkers. They think in terms of intangibles like timing, morale, attitude, momentum, and atmosphere. They read between the lines. They anticipate the unexpected.

LEADERS THINK QUICKLY

Leaders size up a situation quickly and then seize it immediately. Two reasons leaders are able to do this are that they think in terms of the big picture, and they do their homework so that they have information to use to help them make decisions quickly.

As Dan developed as a leader, he took on a tremendous amount of the load for me. He ran Skyline for me, directly led thirteen pastors, and oversaw a staff of more than forty. But Dan did more than that. Where he most excels is in the development of other men. Since 1987, Dan has selected a handful of men each year to personally develop. Already he has worked with and developed more than one hundred of them.

Dan's development of leaders is systematic and strategic. He constantly looks for potential leaders to develop, and he sees himself as a lightning rod, able to capture and focus the energy required to make men grow. For his part, he says he is effective because he always keeps in mind the *vision* of developing leaders, he maintains people development as a *lifestyle*, and he renews his *commitment* to it regularly. The key to the whole process, though, is relationships. He says that the men he develops grow as leaders due to their relationships with one another, the equipping that they receive, and the synergy of their interaction with him and one another. What sustains the whole process, though, is the relational part of it—the area in which he himself has grown the most.

A LEADER CHANGES LEADERSHIP STYLE

When I hired Sheryl Fleisher on my Skyline staff, I knew she was a strong leader. She had vision, was able to make decisions, thought big, and had a bottom-line mentality. But she also tended to be autocratic and a bit dogmatic. She was a leader, but she did not lead relationally. She described herself as having been "mission-minded" rather than "people-minded."

The turning point in Sheryl's development came when she handled a difficult situation with a person less effectively than she could have. She describes the way she did things as "politically naïve and relationally stupid." Soon after it happened, I sat down with her and told her that I supported her and believed in her but that she would have to grow and change her leadership style if she wanted to make it on the team. Not only did she grow as a leader, she became one of the team's best leaders.

With Sheryl, my goal was not to change her personality. It was to change her mode of operation, her style of leadership. She relied on structure and position to establish her leadership. I wanted her to become a relational/empowering leader. There were times that I had to stop what I was doing and do some backtracking to retrain her, but it was definitely worth the effort. Any time you want to change a leader's style, you must do the following:

MODEL A BETTER LEADERSHIP STYLE

The very first thing you must do is show them your better leadership style. If they don't see that there is a better way to lead, they will never change.

IDENTIFY WHERE THEY ERR

Observe them to determine where they make their mistakes. You won't be able to help them change if you don't know what must be changed.

GET THEIR PERMISSION TO HELP THEM CHANGE

If they are not committed to the process of change and to allowing you to help them, all your effort will be wasted. People will give you their permission when they hurt enough to need change, learn enough to want change, or receive enough to make them able to change.

SHOW THEM HOW TO GET FROM HERE TO THERE

Even when they have the knowledge that they need to change and the desire to make a change, they may not be capable of making a change. Show them the way, step by step.

GIVE IMMEDIATE FEEDBACK

Because you will be helping them break bad habits, you must respond to their actions immediately. Learning something for the first time is always easier than unlearning something that was learned wrong. I learned that lesson when I had to unlearn my golf swing. When you retrain people to lead relationally, give them immediate feedback for both the good things and the bad.

As Sheryl grew and began to lead from the heart, she became a wonderful developer of leaders. She identifies people development as her passion in life. When she became the pastor of personal growth ministries at Skyline, she, like Dan, was always searching for people to develop. She listed the following qualities in the women she was to develop:

F *aithful*	They must be consistent in their actions, reliable, and committed.
A *vailable*	They must be accessible to her personally and willing to grow.
I *nitiating*	They must be inquisitive and hungry to grow.
T *eachable*	They must be receptive to her style of mentoring and teaching.
H *onest*	They must be transparent and honestly willing to develop others.

Sheryl and I once sat down to talk about the way she develops people. I think she lost track of how many people she worked with, but she is very aware of the positive effect her mentoring had on Skyline. She told me that her joy is to recognize where people are, meet them there, love and accept them, and then mentor them. Her goal is to get them to develop into the people they were created by God to be. And she wants to get them to carry on the tradition of leadership development. She succeeds too. She mentioned that one of the women she developed pointed out *six generations of leaders* in one room who had been mentored starting with Sheryl. That's quite an accomplishment. Today Sheryl continues to make an impact as a staff member of Willow Creek Community Church.

A GOOD LEADER BECOMES A GREAT LEADER

Dick Peterson was already a first-class leader before he met me. When I came to Skyline, he was a manager in what was America's premier corporation at the time—IBM. In fact, Dick was one of the top three managers in the country in IBM's administrative area. Had he stayed with IBM, his next step would have been to regional management, then on to a vice presidency. And I'm sure he would have made it. As a leader, he was probably in the top 5 percent in the country.

When I had been at Skyline for about a year, I asked him to become a member of the church board. I wanted him on the team. I knew he would be a great contributor to the church and me, and I believed he would also benefit from the experience. You see, I give more thought, time, and attention to the development of the people on my board than to anyone else, with the exception of my family. Board members are the top leaders and influencers I have contact with.

I spent three years developing Dick while he was on the board. I built a good personal relationship with him, I spent time equipping him, and I constantly challenged him to grow. Once when I was preparing to fly to Dallas to talk to some people about ways to begin equipping leaders on a larger scale, I took Dick with me. He was a part of the discussion that gave birth to INJOY. As a leader, he jumped right in and helped get it off the ground. He started as a volunteer. He later resigned at IBM to run INJOY full time for more than a decade.

One of the beauties of developing a person who is already a strong leader is that it gives you momentum. Where a leader must *slow down* to develop followers, *stop* to develop managers, and *backtrack* to change the style of misguided leaders, he can actually *speed up* as he strengthens good leaders. They practically teach themselves. They pick things up just by being around you, often with little to no effort on your part.

If you are fortunate enough to have strong leaders in your influence, begin developing them by doing the following:

PUT THEM ON A PERSONAL PLAN FOR GROWTH

Most good leaders are growing, but they frequently do not have a personal plan for growth. After you have gotten to know them—their strengths, weakness, desires, goals, etc.—sit down with them and prepare a personal growth plan tailored to them. Then follow up periodically to encourage them, check their progress, and help them make adjustments.

CREATE OPPORTUNITIES TO STRETCH THEM

It is while doing activities that we thought were beyond our capabilities that our greatest growth occurs. It actually accelerates our development. It also gives us additional opportunities to apply the principles we are learning. As you further develop leaders, plan to put them in situations that will stretch them.

LEARN FROM THEM

Whenever I spend time developing someone who is already a good leader, I learn too. You will also learn much from leaders as long as you maintain a teachable attitude. Plan shared projects with them. It's a great way to learn and to get tremendous things accomplished at the same time.

Dick's development has transformed him. He was already a strong leader, but now he is a strong builder of leaders. Developing people is now like breathing to him. Without it, he wouldn't be who he is. That is the key to developing the leaders around you. As a leader, you must make the development of others a lifestyle. When you live it, your success in life is multiplied exponentially. Your influence is expanded incredibly beyond your personal reach. A positive future is assured for you. Leaders who do not develop people will one day find themselves hitting a wall in their success. No matter how efficient and strategic they are, eventually they run out of time.

I found that to be true in my life. I cannot personally create more material than I am currently creating. I cannot mentor more people than I am presently mentoring. I cannot travel and do more conferences than I do now. I am a very energetic person, but I have reached my own physical limits. The only way I can now do more is by doing it through other people. Any leader who learns that lesson and makes it a lifestyle will never hit the wall again.

So I ask you, are you developing the leaders around you?

NOTES

CHAPTER ONE

1. Tom Worsham, "Are You a Goose?" *The Arizona Surveyor*, 1992.

CHAPTER TWO

1. Edwin Markham, "Man Making"

CHAPTER THREE

1. John C. Maxwell, *The Winning Attitude: Your Key to Personal Success* (Nashville, Tennessee: Thomas Nelson, 1993).

CHAPTER FOUR

1. David A. Seamands, *Healing Grace* (Wheaton, Illinois: Victor Books, 1988).

2. *Success Unlimited* (Magazine no longer in print).

CHAPTER FIVE

1. Bobb Biehl, *Increasing Your Leadership Confidence* (Sisters, Oregon: Questar, 1989).

CHAPTER NINE

1. Florence Littauer, *Personality Plus* (Grand Rapids, Michigan: Revel, 1994).

BOOKS BY DR. JOHN C. MAXWELL CAN TEACH
YOU HOW TO BE A **REAL** SUCCESS

RELATIONSHIPS
> *Becoming a Person of Influence* (Nelson Business)
> *Relationships 101* (Nelson Business)
> *The Treasure of a Friend* (J. Countryman)
> *25 Ways to Win with People* (Nelson Business)
> *Winning with People* (Nelson Business)

EQUIPPING
> *Developing the Leaders Around You* (Nelson Business)
> *Equipping 101* (Thomas Nelson, available January 2004)
> *Partners in Prayer* (Nelson Business)
> *The 17 Essential Qualities of a Team Player* (Nelson Business)
> *The 17 Indisputable Laws of Teamwork* (Nelson Business)
> *Success One Day at a Time* (J. Countryman)
> *Your Road Map for Success* (Nelson Business)

ATTITUDE
> *The Choice is Yours* (J. Countryman)
> *Failing Forward* (Nelson Business)
> *Living at the Next Level* (Nelson Business)
> *Success One Day at a Time Journal* (J. Countryman)

LEADERSHIP
> *Developing the Leader Within You* (Nelson Business)
> *Leadership Promises for Every Day* (J. Countryman)
> *The Right to Lead* (J. Countryman)
> *The 360 Degree Leader* (Nelson Business)
> *The 21 Indispensable Qualities of a Leader* (Nelson Business)
> *The 21 Irrefutable Laws of Leadership* (Nelson Business)
> *The 21 Most Powerful Minutes in a Leader's Day* (Nelson Business)

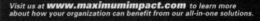

ORGANIZATIONAL PROFILE
maximumimpact™

www.maximumimpact.com

MAXIMUM IMPACT ™ HAS 5 CHANNELS OF CUSTOMER ENGAGEMENT

Corporate Training

Customized Training Solutions for you and your team. We offer open-enrollment, on-location, and train-the-trainer formats. For more details go to: **www.maximumimpact.com/training**

Events

Powerful conferences with incredible speaker line-ups. Past speakers have included: Rudy Giuliani, Ken Blanchard, Jack Welch, Marcus Buckingham, Bobby Bowden, and more! For more details go to: **www.maximumimpact.com/conferences**

Subscriptions

Leadership develops daily, not in a day. Leadership disciplines and habits require constant attention. Our subscription-based monthly mentoring delivers training to you in the form of an audio CD. Go to: **www.maximumimpact.com/monthlyaudio**

Resources

Thousands of topical resources, books, training kits (DVD), audio CDs, web resources, and more. Just what you need to grow as a business and sales leader or as a strong team. For more details go to: **www.maximumimpact.com/resources**

Speakers

Keynote, half-day, and full-day presentations by America's best-known authorities tailored to your organization's needs. For more details go to: **www.maximumimpact.com/speakers**

Visit us at **www.maximumimpact.com** to learn more about how your organization can benefit from our all-in-one solutions.

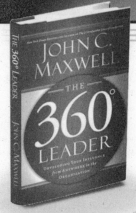

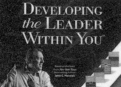
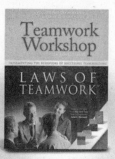

John Maxwell's
REAL
Leadership Series

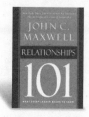

RELATIONSHIPS 101
ISBN 0-7852-6351-9

EQUIPPING 101
ISBN 0-7852-6352-7

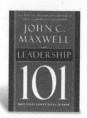

ATTITUDE 101
ISBN 0-7852-6350-0

LEADERSHIP 101
ISBN 0-7852-6419-1

NELSON BOOKS
A Division of Thomas Nelson Publishers
Since 1798

DEVELOPING THE LEADERS AROUND YOU NOTES

DEVELOPING THE LEADERS AROUND YOU NOTES

_____

_____

_____

_____

_____

_____

_____

_____

_____

_____

_____

_____

_____

_____

_____

_____

_____

_____

_____

_____

_____

_____

_____

DEVELOPING THE LEADERS AROUND YOU NOTES

DEVELOPING THE LEADERS AROUND YOU NOTES